El   y

ɔ 2005

THE POLITICAL ECOLOGIST

To our parents and our children.

The Political Ecologist

DAVID WELLS
Senior Lecturer in Politics
University of New England
TONY LYNCH
Lecturer in Philosophy
University of New England

Ashgate

Aldershot • Brookfield USA • Singapore • Sydney

Published by
Ashgate Publishing Ltd
Gower House
Croft Road
Aldershot
Hants GU11 3HR
England

Ashgate Publishing Company
Old Post Road
Brookfield
Vermont 05036
USA

Ashgate website: http://www.ashgate.com

British Library Cataloguing in Publication Data
Wells, David
    The political ecologist
    1. Political ecology - Great Britain 2. Environmentalism -
    Great Britain 3. Green movement - Political aspects - Great
    Britain
    I. Title II. Lynch, Tony
    322.4'0941

Library of Congress Catalog Card Number: 99-76343

ISBN 0 7546 1119 1

Printed in Great Britain by
Antony Rowe Ltd, Chippenham, Wiltshire

Contents

Introduction

Not everyone today exhibits a concern for the well-being of our shared environment. For some such a concern is simple delusion, for everything is fine, and is going to be fine. We discuss this sanguine denial in the following chapter. But if for most of us the concern is there it is very often swamped, even negated, by a concern for our private environment—the luxury of a car and house, the conditions and possibilities of travel, the opportunities for employment, personal enrichment, and so on. Perhaps this concern for the private environment at the expense of the public is ultimately self-defeating: if there is enough public squalor and neglect then there can be no real private comfort or luxury. But still such a focus is understandable, for it reflects some key features of modernity. So it is that the operations of unfettered capitalism are thought by many to harness private ends to public goods without the need for rules and structures of explicit public concern. The "free" or "socially disembedded" market will ensure that supply and demand are neatly and sustainably matched, not only for manufactured widgets and financial goods, but for natural resources and environmental goods generally; and if there are market-failures, if there are burgeoning "negative externalities", well they too can be met by extending the market into new areas, or quietened by the assumption that "overall" negative externalities will be matched by their positive brothers, so that the effective sum is zero and rightfully omitted from economic calculation.

It is an orthodoxy today that government action on behalf of the public interest is to be viewed with deep suspicion, even hostility. Such intervention and action is stigmatised as inherently incompetent, self-serving and ineffective, even pernicious to the extent that its welfarist implications are felt to undermine "individual enterprise" and "personal responsibility" for the parasitic comforts of the "culture of dependency". Add to this a climate of deepening economic insecurity and destabilising social change in which individuals are increasingly forced to think in the privatised terms of immediate self-interest, and we have a recipe which systematically cuts against explicit and effective public action anywhere, including the protection and provision of environmental goods.

Such a recipe gains further authority because of the seemingly fragmented and "unrealistic" prescriptions for environmental protection and respect pushed by many environmentalists. Those who claim a certain "hard headed realism" look with piteous contempt on "Greenies" who may insist, among other things, that we develop a new "non-anthropocentric" ethic in which natural entities and processes are attributed as much moral standing as anything human; that we replace a socio-political program of economic growth with that of a steady-state, even declining, standard of material well-being; and that we lock up forever natural resources on which the possibilities of escaping poverty for many of the world depend.

Even worse for the environmental movement in the eyes of its critics, is the fact there is no agreement, even amongst the most sincere advocates of environmental protection and concern, on what would constitute a truly green politics. Here views range from the centralised authoritarianism championed by William Ophuls,[1] to the decentralised anarchy propounded by Murray Bookchin[2] and the social ecologist movement; from the "working within the system" approach favoured by human welfare ecologists, to the terroristic directives of those "eco-warriors" influenced by the "Earth First!" movement. But it is not simply diversity alone which weakens the environmentalist's case—after all, diversity can be a boon if it reflects the results of rigorous inquiry—it is the seeming inability of such approaches to give a principled articulation of environmental politics which fits it with continuing concerns for social justice and equity. So, for instance, there is at present in the Australian context a battle within the environmental movement concerning the creation and imposition of private tollways. For some (eg, the Total Environment Centre) such private tollways are desirable because they place an addition cost on vehicular travel, and so discourage a polluting activity; that such a measure is fiscally regressive is thought not to the point; what comes first is the environment, equity at best a distant second. For others (eg, The Australian Greens) such fiscal regression is to be condemned precisely because of its inequitable effects. For the Australian Green Senator Bob Brown, environmental concerns cannot genuinely be realised in or through the production of human injustice.

In sum the critics of environmentalism argue one or all of the following: that explicit environmental concern is unnecessary given that a functional free market economy will provide public benefits more effectively and efficiently than a system of organised public concern; that the environmentalist program is at best, morally, economically and politically unrealistically utopian, and at worst positively pernicious; and that the environmental movement itself is so racked with conflicts and confusions as to be incapable of providing a principled approach to the broader issues of moral and political decision-making.

In this book we aim to provide a satisfying answer to these charges. We develop a comprehensive and coherent politics not only for the environmentally concerned but for all concerned to uncover a "third-way" between the authoritarianism of the centralised state and the brutalities of the unrestricted market. The upshot of our argument is that rightly understood green politics is a form—even the original form—of *Liberal* politics understood as an encompassing concern for the sustaining background conditions of a flourishing social life. Such a concern is not directly a concern with what people want—wants occupy the political and personal foreground—but with what they *need* so as to have the possibility of such a foreground. We call this "third way", this needs-based politics of the background, *Political Ecology*, and its novelty lies neither with environmentalism or with liberalism alone, but in their essential conjunction. For while opposition to environmentalism comes from many quarters, conservative and socialist as well as liberal, it is the liberal critique of the public dimension environmentalism implies which today carries the most force. We think this critique is mistaken on its own terms; that it reflects an understandable though regrettable misunderstanding of liberalism itself. For liberal politics, in the hands of its foundational thinker John Locke, just *is* a politics of the background. It arises as a means of dealing effectively with collectively generated environmental failures through the internalisation of risk in the development of systems of communal self-insurance. And while Locke's argument focuses on failures in the human environment—the lack of personal and material security and the generation of vicious cycles of injustice—his "social contract" strategy generalises to the provisions of the natural environment. A point implicit in Garrett Hardin's reading of environmentalism through the parable of "tragedy of the commons".[3]

Our account as it follows is not meant as a liberal polemic. Our kind of liberalism did not pre-exist our environmentalism, rather the exploration of our environmentalism led us to (a now *green*) liberalism in the form of political ecology. In this book we work our way as we ourselves worked our way: from and through a concern for environmental ends, to a newly (re)conceived understanding of the nature and challenges of liberal politics.

Acknowledgements

Thanks to Margaret Wells and Annette Kilarr, and to those students whose enthusiasm and desire for clarity led us to this book.

Notes

1   William Ophuls, *Ecology and the Politics of Scarcity: A Prologue to a Political Theory of the Steady State*, (San Francisco: Freeman, 1972).
2   Murray Bookchin, *The Ecology of Freedom: The Emergence and Dissolution of Hierachy*, (Palo Alto, California: Cheshire, 1982).
3   Garrett Hardin, "The Tragedy of the Commons", *Science*, 1968, Vol. 162, pp. 1243-1248.

1 Why Environmentalism?

If this work starts off with a major assumption it is simply this: we face a range of significant and serious environmental problems. And the "we" referred to here is not just ourselves as individuals, nor even the national populations of which we are a part, but the human species as a whole. For anyone who has taken serious note of environmental issues over the last several decades this is unlikely to be considered a controversial position. If nothing else the frightening figures on the world-wide decline of bio-diversity should be enough to clinch the case. However, even in the face of such overwhelming evidence, it is equally clear that the kind of responses put in place for dealing with these problems are woefully inadequate. Indeed, there is every indication that there has been a retreat, by governments and others, from the kind of environmentally driven policies which might have real impact, to what are often only superficial and media-managed approaches. It is part of the purpose of this book to try to unravel why this is the case, as well as to provide suggestions as to how this state of affairs might be altered. As a start it is useful to look at one of the more obvious aspects of social existence. For whenever social and political life confronts us with pressures and forces which, to the clear sighted, make manifest demands for serious and determined political action, there are also those who, even as the destructive processes strengthen, deny that there is a problem at all, apart, of course, from the problem of those who insist on making such disquieting claims in the first place. We might call this the "Versailles" response in honour of Louis XVI and his celebrated Queen, and it reflects the operation in our thoughts and lives, of what might be called the *Principle of Least Disruption*.

The Principle of Least Disruption is a little noted, but pervasive force in human life, both individually and collectively. It designates the standing propensity of persons to avoid discomfort by denying the need for policies and actions which produce unsettling and difficult demands for the active alteration of circumstances otherwise felt to be quite acceptable. It is, in other words, the *inertial* component of our lives, and while it has a positive role in so far as it stands against wild oscillations in our judgement and actions, it also has its downside. For the inertial principle is not a truth of the world, a

5

deliverance of external reality, but an element of inner reality, a way of organising our thoughts and lives that is useful only to the extent that it does not blind us, as it did with the unfortunate King and Queen, to the real pressures acting on us.

It is important that we do not let the Principle of Least Disruption cloud our appreciation of the environmental challenges we confront. For environmental disasters, and humanly caused environmental disasters, *do* happen, and *have* happened many times before. To insist on this should be unnecessary, but it is not. For example it is not unusual for us as teachers to find students of environmentalism, at least initially, decrying the "hysteria" of environmental critics of modernity on the grounds that "civilisation" has shown that it develops from lower to higher stages so that we, today, are at the cutting edge of an ever progressive process which, on the evidence of history, will doubtless continue in perpetuity. This comforting view remains in the chauvinistic grip of nineteenth century social evolutionism, for by refusing to pluralise "civilisation" or "culture", it ignores real, as opposed to imaginary, history altogether. For civilisations and societies do come and go, and have come and gone. "Progress" is not a universal law, and environmental problems have often played a major, even critical, role in social and cultural collapse and disintegration; just as, on the other hand, environmental resources have proven crucial to social and cultural development.

Consider, in this context, the historical fate of the "fertile crescent", that part of Southwest Asia which now includes the territories of Israel, Jordan, Syria, and parts of Iraq and Turkey. It was here that cities first arose, that writing was developed, and empires formed from around 7000 BC, beginning with the Akkadians under Sargon I, and including later the power and magnificence of Babylon and Persia, and the military developments and terrors of the Hittites and Assyrians. For most scholars this progressive move into urbanised life from small, decentralised village life, was no accident. Certainly it did not "just happen" where it did, as if it could have sprung up just about anywhere on the habitable globe. At the time the fertile crescent, as the name suggests, had the most abundant cropping and domesticable animal resources of any area on earth. It was these unique environmental resources which enabled it to become at that time the "world leader in food production".[1] The nutritional surpluses generated enabled the development of political and cultural elites, able to live off the work of those still bound into nature, to develop armed forces for conquest and consolidation, to engage labour forces for large-scale construction, and to develop systems of increasingly sophisticated religious and cosmological speculation.

If the environmental riches of the fertile crescent help account for the emergence of these first civilisations, why, as Jared Diamond asks, does the subsequent history of western civilisations see the locus of development and power shift away from the fertile crescent and into western and northern Europe? His answer should give pause to those tempted to endorse the optimism of our relaxed students:

> The major factor behind these shifts becomes obvious as soon as one compares the modern fertile crescent with ancient descriptions of it. Today, the expressions "Fertile Crescent" and "world leader in food production" are absurd. Large areas of the former fertile crescent are now desert, semidesert, steppe, or heavily eroded or salinized terrain unsuited for agriculture. Today's ephemeral wealth of some of the region's nations, based on the single nonrenewable resource of oil, conceals the region's long-standing fundamental poverty and difficulty in feeding itself. In ancient times, however, much of the fertile crescent and eastern Mediterranean region, including Greece, was covered with forest. The region's transformation from fertile woodland to eroded scrub or desert has been elucidated by palaeobiologists and archaeologists. Its woodlands were cleared for agriculture, or cut to obtain construction timber, or burned as firewood or for manufacturing plaster. Because of low rainfall and hence low primary productivity (proportional to rainfall), regrowth of vegetation could not keep pace with its destruction, especially in the presence of overgrazing by abundant goats. With the tree and grass cover removed, erosion proceeded and valleys silted up, while irrigation agriculture in the low rainfall environment led to salt accumulation...
>
> Thus, Fertile Crescent and eastern Mediterranean societies had the misfortune to arise in an ecologically fragile environment. *They committed ecological suicide by destroying their resource base.*[2]

Far from "ecological suicide" being an impossibility for a civilisation, it has been a crucial component of the end of many stories, and so—it is an obvious induction, even without the markers of environmental deterioration that surround us—perhaps of *our* story. What differences there are between the past and today provide no reason for optimism, quite the contrary. For if the civilisations of the fertile crescent declined as environmental poverty and damage accumulated, the skills and capacities in plant and animal domestication they developed could be, and were, taken on by other societies elsewhere. But in key respects our environmental story is today irredeemably global, and increasingly so with every passing moment. In our case, the "ecological suicide" many fear would not merely threaten chunks of the world (though it certainly does that), but the whole shebang.

The second point to make is more subtle. It is a further consequence of the Principle of Least Disruption that for many of us the apparent lack of uniform agreement—even between acknowledged "experts"—on the necessity for significant and meaningful change, often functions as a reason for denying the very idea. Thus, for instance, while the Intergovernmental Panel on Climate Change (IPCC), a body of 2,500 scientific experts set up by the United Nations, has stated that "the balance of evidence suggests that there is a discernible human influence on global climate", and recommends determined action to slow, halt, and hopefully reduce greenhouse gas emissions, it is enough for some to find a contrary view, even if held by someone or some body whose ulterior interests are by no means obscure, by which to dismiss the very idea. Of course a modicum of conservatism is crucial to scientific progress, but when conservatism, under the influence of the Principle of Least Disruption, becomes reactionary, then any kind of progress, any kind of science, becomes impossible.

The more sophisticated of the reactionaries contend that their position is nothing more than an example of another principle, the so-called "Precautionary Principle" which environmentalists themselves often appeal to in order to oppose certain policies and practices, but the claim is mistaken. The precautionary principle is not a principle of uniformity, so that only if everyone (at least, everyone "competent") agrees on the likely outcome of some process, should we operate on the assumption that that will be the outcome. Rather the precautionary principle is a principle of *collective prudence.* In particular it holds that if there is significant disagreement between experts on the reality or nature of some threatening phenomenon—as is to be expected on complex and difficult issues—and this phenomenon, under one of the competing interpretations, promises or threatens the difference between a general *safety* and *catastrophe,* then we should not blithely accept the risk of the latter, but, as a matter of decent self-interest, do all we can to avoid or avert the risk.

The lesson thus far is that it is wrong to reject environmentally based calls for changes in our patterns of impact on the world on the grounds either that there is no evidence for such potential catastrophe, nor the lack of universal agreement on the reality of such changes. Both claims are unfortunate but expected consequences of the tendency to allow our lives to ruled by the Principle of Least Disruption.

Finally, we mention the most perverse expression of the Principle, for though it is utterly bankrupt it features many times in contemporary assaults on environmentalism. Whereas the first expression of the principle argues for the infallibility of civilisation as an agent for progressive development, now the thought seems to be that if the environmental impacts "civilisation" produces lie within the range of possible "natural variation", then even though those changes are doubtless occurring, no remedial action on our part is required. We find the clearest example of this peculiar conviction in the case of global warming. For there are those, including a number of scientists, who rest a case for policy quietism on the grounds that the present and anticipated levels of warming and sea level rise are within the range of historically determined "natural variation".

The fallacy is twofold. First, the claim of "natural variation" should give no comfort, for much of terrestrial history—indeed virtually all of it—not only occurred before the human presence, but under conditions which would (and did) render human life impossible. It is, for example, within the range of "natural variation" to have an atmosphere with virtually no oxygen. Equally, cataclysmic impacts from extra-terrestrial bodies are within that "natural range". In neither case should this reassure us of the humanly benign consequences of a deoxygenated world, or one blasted by a major extra-terrestrial impact. The problem is that such claims avoid matters of aetiology, of the causal processes which explain the observed changes. Thus since the mid-nineteenth century the atmospheric levels of CO_2, the major greenhouse gas, have risen around 30%, from 280 to 362 parts per million, their highest level for 150,000 years. We may be as yet "within the range of natural variation", but this time there is reason to think the variation is underpinned by novel human processes. Policy quietism towards environmental change is not the upshot of a sane "historical realism", but an exercise in fatalism. The argument takes the following form: Either the world will get too hot to sustain human society, or it will not. If the former is true, then remedial action is useless, and if the latter is true, it is unnecessary. This call to blissful thoughtlessness has perennial inertial attraction, but consider the following: either I will pass this exam or I will not; if I do, then studying for it is unnecessary, and if I don't then studying for it is useless. As with all expressions of fatalism, the fallacy lies in ignoring to the point of absurdity the role of human judgement and decision in determining the lines of future history. In the end it expresses little more than an irresponsible abdication of personal and social responsibility.

Having exposed the misguided operations of the Principle of Least Disruption, it is surely true today, as perhaps never before, that we confront the operations of environmental forces with more than enough power to shake the inertial grip of the *status quo*; or rather, of the increasingly nostalgic idea of the *status quo*. After all, never before have there been so many people in the world making demands, typically increasing demands, on natural systems and resources; and never before has there been such an array of increasingly complex techniques and processes available for the exploitation of environmental goods.

The frequency and scale of traditional problems such as pollution, for instance, is undeniably far beyond anything humanity has yet generated. Doubtless there have been oil spills and the production of toxic emissions from burning oil, ever since its discovery, but there have not been billions of internal combustion engines, massive supertankers, or millions of kilometres of oil lines criss-crossing the earth. Equally while it is true that all forms of human productive activity have waste implications, the situation is radically altered when local low level technologies are replaced by the sophisticated and massive industrialisation which characterises the present era. So it is that only under modern conditions is there the need and the techniques available to produce in pesticide production such frightening substances as the methyl isocyanate which, in 1984, escaped from the Union Carbide factory in Bhopal, India, killing 4,000, disabling 30,000, and affecting the health of up to 180,000 people. Nor has there been the possibility of such accidents as that at the Chernobyl Nuclear Complex in 1987, when a nuclear reactor meltdown released on a continental scale such appalling and novel toxins as Plutonium, Iodine-131, Strontium-90 and Caesium-137.

The very scale of the singular accident at Chernobyl shows us that in many areas we are entering unchartered waters. If, despite their sometimes devastating consequences, previous environmental disasters were essentially local in form, today it is hard to read any environmental problem as essentially local. Even to understand properly such an ostensibly personal and minor issue as littering involves us in considerations of packaging and marketing in the context of emerging global capitalism, just as to understand the nature of the disaster at Bhopal involves like considerations in the context of a technologically driven "Green Revolution" aimed at dealing with the nutritional demands of continually increasing population. Equally, there are immediately global issues, of which we have mentioned already greenhouse gas induced global warming, but there are others, from the continuing depletion of the Ozone layer and the massive reduction in biodiversity, to the recent discovery of drastically falling male fertility rates across nations which many experts attribute to endocrine disruption attributable to the actions of certain synthetic chemical compounds.

We could, at this point, take the route of the Ehrlichs and attempt to scare the pants off the reader by introducing the ever increasing scientific literature on such matters, including now such things as desertification, soil erosion and salinization, deforestation, water scarcity, acid rain, the decline of fisheries and plateauing of agricultural productiveness, the increasing expense and ineffectiveness of antibiotic drugs as both old and new infectious diseases extend their often fatal reach, and so on down an ever extending list. But as we are not natural scientists, and as such consideration can be found elsewhere, most notably in the careful research and regular publications of the World Watch Institute, we will not fling figures at the reader here. Besides, there is always the danger that without presenting those ideas and strategies which promise to make such difficulties commensurable with the possibilities of human remediation, that the reader returns exhausted to the short-term, but undeniable, pleasures of a comfortable inertia, or, if that is no longer a genuine possibility, at least into the quietistic fatalism which lets everything go on as before, regardless of the consequences.

In the following chapters we show how to comprehend and deal with the environmental challenges we face. But for those who remain sceptical of the dangers we confront today, preferring instead, to place all trust in the managerial powers of unreconstructed modernity, we draw attention to the path-breaking work of Ulrich Beck,[3] Professor at the Institute for Sociology at Ludwig-Maximilians University, Munich. Beck is a sociologist, not a natural scientist, and his understanding of our environmental challenges and threats does not, as it does for the WorldWatch Institute, rely directly on scientific research. Instead Beck's argument works on the chosen plane of our inertial defenders of environmental quietism. For he contends that it is already becoming clear in the "modern industrial system" that things environmental are spinning from our control. Rather than appealing to contested scientific data to defend his view, he draws attention instead to the signs of an emerging *operational* breakdown within the self-regulatory systems of industrial society itself. It is at these points that the environment has begun to break through the limits of managerial control.

Rather than denigrating the achievements of industrial society, Beck begins by celebrating its achievements. He points out that traditional societies faced many *external* threats—plagues, famines, sickness, and so on. These threats were beyond the powers of understanding and technological capacities of such societies. They were not, or were not understood as, the results of human decisions. They were rather "acts of the gods". It followed that the only rational approach to management was to seek a good relationship with the gods through the rituals of sacrifice. But today things are different; indeed are different in a way that gives an initial force to the anti-environmental position. For it is part of that "progress" which recommends the *status quo* that many threats that were once thought of as external, now are thought of as *internal*. For instance mortality rates are held to depend not simply on the incalculable luck of individuals, but in part on the calculable patterns of automobile safety and driving habits, and on the effectiveness or otherwise of public health policy, etc. Here, what was once invariably external, a bolt from the outside, is now in large part internal, a matter of human action and decision.

As Beck tells the story of modern industrial society, it is—for an extended period, at least—one of progressive control of the environment. In particular it is a matter of turning traditional threats into *risks*, and of dealing with the new insecurities and potential destructiveness of our patterns and techniques of material production so they too are internalised as risks, and so open to "supra-individual, political rules of recognition, settlement and avoidance". The paradigmatic element of this internalisation is the insurance contract. By turning consequences that once simply bore down on the isolated individual or group into actuarially calculated risks, threats become merely occasions for effective risk-management. Rather than threatening the stability and continuity of the industrial society, they strengthen and further its ends of managed control in the service of economic and social well-being.

The advantages to this insurance based strategy of internalisation are hard to underestimate, for it means that individuals are freed from a whole range of potentially crushing burdens that otherwise they would face all alone. The statistical documentation and calculation of risks in problematic areas of social life, from smoking to nuclear power, from the economic risks of unemployment, illness and old age, to the natural vulnerability to flood and hurricanes, reveals that even in the latter cases the deleterious consequences are in part conditioned by the system (eg, by building standards, land zoning decisions, irrigation strategies, coastal management programs, energy policy, pollution regulations, etc.) and so call for general political regulation.

Further than this, the internalisation of threats as risks through insurance opens up the incentive for preventative strategies. Thus a non-smoker can expect to pay lower premiums on their life-insurance policy, just as a home owner might expect to pay more if he insists, and is allowed, to build in an area prone to flooding, or a farmer to pay more in third party insurance if he relies on dangerous pesticides and insecure methods of delivery. There is a positive feedback mechanism involved in the internalisation of risks which works to reduce the very need for insurance in the first place. The world becomes not more, but less dangerous as industrial society becomes more deeply established.

This leads to the third positive aspect of industrial society's internalisation of risk. For by subjecting risks to insurance based strategies of management industrial society is enabled to deal with its own unforeseeable future. As Beck puts it: "The calculus of risks and protection by insurance promises the impossible: events that have not yet occurred can be addressed now—through prevention, compensation, or provisions for after-care." Out of the warp and woof of private and public insurance the industrial system developed a system of "social contracts" which create present security and encourage future security in the face of uncertainty. This is no mean achievement.

Just as, in Chapter Three, we shall see how misguided it is for environmentalists to run up the banner of zero or negative economic growth, it is equally misguided to diminish or demean industrial society's capacity for risk management. Those environmentalists who assume a blanket hostility to all things modern give perverse endorsement to their equally determined opponents; for only those safely cloistered in a world of risk management could possibly call for a return to the world of external threats which loomed over premodern societies. Effective risk management is a good thing and is not to be disparaged. For Beck, however, environmentalism arises precisely at those points where effective risk management is failing. For the very system of "social contracts" which holds our risk society together is unmistakably unravelling under the developing hazards of "nuclear, chemical, genetic, and ecological megahazards." When risks become megahazards, then the calculus of risk unravels in four ways.

First, these disasters often threaten irreparable harm on a continental or global scale, harms that effectively are no longer limited in scope or range, and thus the concept of monetary compensation fails. Second, for the worst imaginable accidents the results are fatal on an unprecedented scale. And, of course, for the dead there is no provision for, and no hope of, after-care, and so the security concept of monitoring results fails. Next, with megahazards the "accident" loses its circumscribed location in time and space, and therefore its meaning. It becomes an "event" with a beginning and no end; it becomes an "open-ended carnival of galloping, creeping, overlapping waves of destruction." But this implies, fourth, that the standards of normality, the actuarial techniques for the calculation of risk, collapse. At this point calculation loses its capacity for reassurance (as it does, for example, with nuclear risks), and turns instead into simple obfuscation.

When environmental risks are beyond the calculus of risk, then we have again re-entered the world of the threat-society, though now a world which promises more than the merely local disasters which threatened, and sometimes sank, many premodern societies.

It is the very point of the scientific research and literature we spoke of above, that we are facing all kinds of potential megahazards, most fundamentally the threat of ecological suicide on a terrestrial scale. But as we have seen, there are those, not always entirely without reason, who deny the practical import of such theoretically informed findings. It is for them in particular, and as a beachhead to the wider problems, that Beck points to the ways that modern industrial society is failing on its own terms. "There is", he writes, "an operational criterion to distinguish between risks and threats... *Business itself identifies the limit of tolerability with economic precision by refusing to offer private insurance."*

Many areas of life, and areas for life, are uninsurable today, and they are increasing. Thus certain kinds of life, health and property insurance may be unavailable to you because of your inherited genetic makeup, your postcode, or the low-lying nature of the land you occupy. The risk of ill health or theft or flooding becomes a threat, just as it was in the hunter-gather group. Equally, whole industries and industrial practices operate without private insurance, relying (if relying on anything at all) on the government or the "international community" to pick up the tab.

Equally to the point is the 1996 decision of some sixty of the world's largest insurance companies to sign a statement urging the world's national governments to ensure reduced greenhouse gas emissions. The costs of insurance against natural disasters have risen to levels that the companies find increasingly unsustainable on purely commercial grounds. In 1996, damage from weather-related disasters reached a record 60 billion US dollars, a record broken in each successive year. Indeed, according to Munich Re, one of the biggest reinsurance companies in the world, "Comparing the figures for the 1960s and the past ten years [1988-1998], we have established that the number of great natural catastrophes was three times larger. The cost to the world's economies, after adjusting for inflation, is nine times higher and for the insurance industry three times as much." And it has done so, according to Gerhard Berz, head of geoscience research at Munich Re, because of higher temperatures and greater storm intensity causally connected with human-induced global warming.[4]

If, even from within the perspective of modern industrial society, we can discern the emerging operational breakdown in the calculus of risks and the emergence of threats, then we cannot avoid the conclusion that the *status quo* is unsustainable. While it is puerile to respond, as do too many environmentalists, with unstructured or utopian calls for "total change", it is certain that there are major implications for politics. What was at stake in the old industrial conflict of labour against capital were largely *positives:* profits, prosperity, consumer goods. In the new ecological conflict, on the other hand, often what is at stake are *negatives*: losses, devastation, threats. This change from a politics that emphasises positives, to that which dwells on the negatives, poses a number of serious questions, of which two stand out.

The first question is an ancient one. How can we deal with a politics which is often engaged in negative-sum and zero-sum conflicts, without giving it a decidedly authoritarian cast? Agreement is easy (or at least *easier*) to obtain when everyone gains, or thinks that they will gain, from the deal. Positive conflict is like this. Everyone is to gain, the question is by how much. At the very least such conditions are favourable to democracy. But with negative conflict, when even in the best case some are certainly going to be worse off, and often precisely to the extent that some others are better-off, it is not so clear that the conditions favour democracy. As a matter of fact we think that a recognisable form of democracy, liberal democracy, does have the resources to deal with such a politics, and often by the more desirable route of transforming such negative-based conflicts into positive sum games, as well as sustaining legitimacy when losses are certain. In a later chapter we show how Lockean liberalism, conceived in terms of its social commons foundations, constitutes a system of communal self-insurance directed at solving effectively problems of scarcity; though Locke, and for understandable reasons, focussed on scarcity of the distributional goods of security from our fellows violence, and the provision of social justice, rather than the secure provision of those even more fundamental environmental goods on which all else depends.

The second question arises not simply from the politics of negative conflict, but from the way it has developed and presented itself to modernity. The self-induced threats we confront threaten, in Beck's striking words, to "render us headless". The following is taken from his reflections on the Chernobyl disaster:

From one day to the next, Chernobyl made conscious what has already been true for a long time: not just in the nuclear age, but with the industrial universalisation of chemical poisons in the air, the water, and foodstuffs as well, our relation to reality has been fundamentally transformed. To use a famous analogy, private control over the means of perception has been overthrown. The senses have been expropriated—in all the splendour of their images of reality.

The invisibility of the causes, and (often) the effects of such contamination means that in our judgements and decisions "we are continually at the mercy of social institutions: weather services, mass media, cabinet officers, officially determined tolerance levels, etc". The danger is that accountability lapses. When neither cause nor effect is open to individual assessment, but demands the expertise of an elite, then democratic monitoring and assessment is impossible or "irrational". Beck continues:

> In nuclear democracy, we the citizens have lost sovereignty over our senses and thus the residual sovereignty over our judgement ... we have been reduced to media products in the bright glare of our education or ignorance. The disempowerment of our senses forces us into a situation in which we must accept the dictation of centralised information which can at best be relativised in the interplay of contradictions.

What then, can be done to domesticate, and in a politically acceptable way, the emerging threats of environmental megahazards? For Beck:

> The key to combating destruction of the environment is not found in the environment itself, nor in a different individual morality or in different research or business ethics; by nature *it lies in the regulatory systems of the institutions* that are becoming historically questionable.

If the problems are finally problems of, and for, "regulatory systems", then this is where environmentalism and environmental politics in particular must focus. Drawing on Garrett Hardin's environmental parable, "the tragedy of the commons", we argue that the right focus takes a recognisable liberal form, for only something along the lines of a "social contract" solution to the problems Beck brings to our attention promises to be effective. Beck himself does not go deeply into these questions, offering instead a list of policy recommendations, each aimed at re-internalising the threats cast up by human action and decision. But it is all very well to offer such suggestions, it is another thing for them, or something like them, to inform political thought and practice. Beck's account lacks a political philosophy, and without it regulatory reform looks *ad hoc*, or just too difficult. But what political philosophy ought the environmentalist embrace? For many, even most, avowed environmental writers the answer is something *new*. The most radical—self-ascribed "deep ecologists"—argue that ethical humanism itself is a mistake, and that the new politics must respect the principle of "biocentric equality", or "ecocentrism", according to which all living things, or all functional elements of an ecosystem, bear an equal moral value. We discuss this proposal in the next chapter. In the subsequent chapter we consider the more moderate and certainly more widespread view that the new politics is characterised by its fundamental hostility towards economic growth, and the politics of such growth.

Notes

1   Jared Diamond, *Guns, Germs and Steel: The Fates of Human Societies*, (London: Jonathan Cape, 1997), pp. 410-411.
2   *Ibid.*, pp. 41-42. Our italics.
3   Cf. U. Beck, *Ecological Politics in an Age of Risk*, (Cambridge: Polity Press, 1990), and U. Beck, *Ecological Enlightenment*, (New Jersey: Humanities Press, 1991). The quotes from Beck which follow are drawn from the latter work.
4   *The Australian*, 31/12/98, p. 8.

2 Green Politics and Deep Ecological Ethics

Among recent, and not so recent writers on the ecological crisis there are a significant proportion who argue that the solution to our environmental problems requires more than the kind of reformist *political* solution foreshadowed in the previous chapter, it requires rather a revolutionary revision of the very *ethical* basis of our civilisation. According to this view the *ultimate* cause of the long process of environmental degradation can be traced to the dominance of a particular ethical orientation to the non-human environment— an ethic which is deeply embedded in western culture—and it is only when this ethic is repudiated that there can be any hope for the creation of an ecologically viable society.

In particular, the "anthropocentric" or "humanist" bias of western culture is identified as the source of the problem. While-ever, the argument goes, we continue to perceive the world from a stand-point which places humans at the centre of creation and relegates other forms of life to a secondary position then, whatever our political tinkerings, we will simply perpetuate the attitudes to nature which have led to our past mistakes. What is required for us to move beyond the insightful but still superficial responses of the kind Beck recommends, is a rejection of the anthropocentric perspective which dominates our culture and its replacement by an ethical perspective which gives equal significance to all forms of life in the workings of our world. Rather than humanism constituting the full flowering of ethical consciousness, the dangers it constitutes for human survival itself, let alone the danger and harm it visits on other living things, indicate the need to move beyond what is, essentially, just a parochial moral perspective. As an alternative we must embrace as our moral foundation the principle of "biocentric equality".

The diagnoses offered for the humanist moral bias of western civilisation follow generally along one of two paths, though the upshot of taking each is the shared commitment to the principle of biocentric equality. In an influential and oft quoted essay the cultural historian Lynn White Jr. argues that "the historical roots of our ecological crisis" lie in the Judeo-Christian world-view which proposes as a basic axiom the idea that "nature has no reason for existence save to serve man".[1] "Western Christianity is the most anthropocentric religion the world has seen" and "the victory of Christianity over paganism was the greatest psychic revolution in the history of our culture". It was this victory which "by destroying pagan animism ... made it possible to exploit nature in a mood of indifference to the feelings of natural objects". This desacralised view of the relationship between humans and nature fuelled the development of modern science and technology, giving Europeans the power to dominate both other cultures and the natural world, and it is the extent of this power which has led to our current situation. The "roots" of our ecological crisis, therefore, are essentially religious and require a religious solution. As a source of such a potential conversion White sees some hope in Asian religions, and particularly Zen Buddhism, but believes that the West is so thoroughly a Christian culture that it must look to Christian radicals like Saint Francis of Assisi, whose "view of nature and of man rested on a unique sort of pan-psychism of all things animate and inanimate", for inspirations appropriate to the development of a new, ecologically benign, culture.

The second diagnostic path for the fundamentally anthropocentric character of western culture and the destructive effect it has had on the environment is to be found in the pioneering work of the deep ecological philosopher Arne Naess who points to the development of "technocratic-industrial" culture as the villain of the piece.[2] The "dominant world-view of technocratic-industrial societies which regards humans as isolated and fundamentally separate from the rest of Nature, as superior to, and in charge of, the rest of creation", involves an historically developed blindness to the moral axiom that "all organisms and entities in the ecosphere, as parts of the interrelated whole, are equal in intrinsic worth". Among the practical conclusions drawn from this "deep ecological" intuition of the moral primitiveness of biocentric equality are the "basic principles" that "humans have no right to reduce ... (the) ... richness and diversity (of the natural world) except to satisfy *vital* needs", and that "the flourishing of nonhuman life requires ... a decrease (in the human population)". Like White, Naess suggests that certain forms of Christianity and Buddhism "provide a fitting background ... for deep ecology". "Deep ecology" provides a "total view" which "can provide a single motivating force for all the activities and movements aimed at saving the planet from human exploitation and domination".

It would not be unfair to say that the development of these kinds of themes has become a major (possibly even *the* major) concern of theoretically inclined environmentalists. William Grey, for example, suggests that "the search for a credible non-anthropocentric basis for value in nature has been the central preoccupation of environmental philosophy".[3] Certainly, a great deal has been written, and the debate between various versions of anthropocentric and biocentric (or, more recently, *ecocentric*) positions shows little sign of abating. Nor has argument remained in the lofty realms of philosophic ethics, it has also had a major impact on Green political theory at all levels. So in the somewhat acrimonious and divisive debate between "Social" and "Deep" Ecologists the question of biocentrism or anthropocentrism has had a central place. The social ecologist Murray Bookchin associates biocentrism with a virulent anti-humanism, suggesting that this kind of view "reduces people from social beings to a simple species—to zoological entities that are interchangeable with bears, bisons, deer, or, for that matter, fruit flies and microbes".[4] Equally, it is the "anthropocentric flavour" of Bookchin's analysis according to which environmental exploitation is finally a manifestation of more fundamental patterns of intra-human exploitation, which forms the basis for many counter-critiques.[5]

More recently, Robyn Eckersley[6] has put forward an ambitious argument for the primacy of an ecocentric approach to Green politics. While allowing that there are a wide range of political positions which can legitimately be regarded as "green", and recognising that the contribution each of these has to make is significant, she nevertheless champions the claims of "an ecocentric philosophical orientation ... [to] ...provide the most comprehensive, promising, and distinctive approach to emancipatory ecopolitical theory". Other views are assessed solely in terms of their anthropocentric/ecocentric character and "to the extent they fall short of a comprehensive ecocentric perspective ... [are] judged inadequate". In contrast to such inadequate views, an ecocentric approach is taken to be "more consistent with ecological reality, more likely to lead us to psychological maturity, and more likely to allow the greatest diversity of beings ... to unfold in their own ways". Furthermore, the development and promotion of ecocentric political theory is vital because "only a thoroughgoing ecocentric Green political theory is capable of providing the kind of comprehensive framework we need to usher in a lasting resolution to the ecological crisis".

In the face of this tradition of a morally pure biocentric equalitarianism within environmentalist thought, a green politics which stresses human welfare and well-being may seem inadequate, even sinful, probably counter-productive, and certainly deserving of the disparaging label—"shallow ecology". On our view, however, there are good reasons to defend what is better called "Human Welfare Ecology" against such charges. It is one thing to argue that the solution to our environmental problems requires significant changes in political outlook and economic activity, or even to recognise that the ultimate product of such changes might well be in many respects a very different social, cultural and ethical life, but quite another to suggest that a fundamental reversal of the underlying ethic of western civilisation is the essential prerequisite for such changes. If "anthropocentrism" is really so basic to our culture and so destructive of the environment, and if it must be replaced with a biocentric or ecocentric ethic in order to create the conditions which will allow us to save the world from ecological devastation, then without doubt we need to go far beyond the traditional politics of human welfare for solutions to our dilemmas. But for all their apparent plausibility, and their appeal to the always attractive fantasy of moral heroism, these are large claims, which deserve critical appraisal.

It is not at all clear, for example, that our treatment of the environment can so readily be attributed to the domination of an anthropocentric Judeo-Christian ethic which gives no value to the natural world. To begin from the obvious: White's claim that Christianity, as opposed to "more primitive" religious attitudes, involves a removal of the sacred from the natural world, and its banishment to the supernatural or transcendent world, leaving behind a nature stripped of any real, any non-instrumental, value may well have some truth in it, but unless the animist's sacrilisation of the natural world generates a system of non exploitative and ecologically harmonious activities, that truth is environmentally irrelevant. That this is in fact the case is suggested by the work of the anthropologist Robin Horton who has spent much of his life investigating the animistic religions of a number of African peoples.[7]

Horton's thesis is that we misunderstand the animist's sacralisation of nature if we see it as reflecting an essentially non-instrumental attitude towards nature. Animistic religions, he argues, while they may have an expressive dimension, are on the deepest level attempts at technological control of an often hostile and threatening world—attempts founded in a respect for nature based more firmly on a human-centred fear than a selfless love of nature. Horton points out that *sacrifice* in the broad sense is the basic feature of animistic religions, and that the purpose of sacrifice is typically to propitiate or to bribe the sacred powers which are, or are in, natural objects. One prays to a deified nature so as to shape its behaviour towards human beings in a way amenable to human interests and purposes. Thus the aim of scientific thinking and animistic religious thinking is essentially the same: to obtain that level of security essential to a worthwhile human existence in a world of scarcity and contingency. The difference lies only in the *kind* of causal explanations each uses. The primitive has typically a limited understanding of the operative causal connections in nature, and certainly when the phenomena extend beyond the most local and immediate as with say, flooding or precipitation patterns, they often lack knowledge of the real causal connections involved; thus in their attempts at providing for their welfare they are led to posit something like human agents in nature, with the hope that the causal connections that operate between human beings can be extended in the interests of control and management into the natural world.

If Horton is right about the shared ends of animistic and scientific thinking—and his ideas are congruent with Beck's discussion of the need to manage risks and deal with threats that all peoples confront—then the primitive, with the sacred in the world, and the Judeo-Christian with it beyond the world, think and act towards nature in the service of much the same human interests; in which case there is no new environmental ethic, no radically new stance towards nature, to be found in resacralising nature.

Equally obvious is the point that the Judeo-Christian heritage in our society is, after all, extraordinarily rich and diverse. To take, as White does, one element of that heritage, to identify it as dominant, and then to attribute the destructive effects of human activities in the environment to it, does seem to overstate the case. Indeed we may wonder at the whole approach, for it involves a touching faith in the connection between Biblical assertion and the thoughts and actions of Western humanity. Certainly it would be extremely welcome if the tight connection deep ecologists perceive in the case of the pronouncements of the Book of Genesis held equally with the even more immediate words of the Sermon on the Mount, but who amongst us would dare affirm that? Furthermore, even if less emphasis is placed on the Judeo-Christian heritage, and more on the development of a "technocratic-industrial" culture, much the same kind of points concerning selectiveness and connection apply.

Consider, for example, the case of Japan. In many ways this can be seen as a society which epitomises the dominance of technocratic-industrial culture, and it is also a society whose record on environmental issues is considerably less than pristine. Yet, it is clear that the foundation of Japanese culture is not in any sense Christian, or even part of the Judeo-Christian heritage. And this is not only a problem for White's argument, it raises equal difficulties for the kind of view put forward by Naess. Even if it were argued that the influence of the Western technocratic-industrial culture on Japanese society during the twentieth century explains the extent of the Japanese impact on the environment, we would still be at a loss to explain why this ethic found such a ready home in a culture whose religious foundation is essentially a mixture of Buddhism and Shinto. If anything, Shinto and the particular variety of Buddhism it has influenced, seems to contain a degree of animism and nature worship which is not so prominent in other variations. At the very least—and leaving aside Horton's arguments which render the apparent universality of nature-exploitation entirely predictable—this indicates that the connection between the fundamental ethic of a society and its impact on the non-human world is not as simple and direct as the environmental critics of western anthropocentrism wish to suggest.

In fact, it is not difficult to find examples of ecological devastation presided over by cultures of almost every variety of religious and ethical belief, and of a manifestly pre- or non- technocratic-industrial nature. The de-afforestation of the fertile crescent was proceeding apace well before the Christian or Islamic eras. Here, and in India, vast tracts of land were degraded by salination through over-irrigation well before the development of "technocratic-industrial" society; just as in China the agricultural, industrial and even religious needs of a growing population over centuries led to the clearing of the great majority of the forest cover with all the subsequent erosion and siltation of the river valleys. It is through his exploration of this last example that the geographer Yi-Fu Tuan[8] is able to draw out some fine ironies in "the gaps that exist between an expressed attitude to the environment and actual practice". Among the most pertinent of these is his account of the environmentally destructive practices often associated with Buddhism. For example, "Buddhism introduced into China the idea of cremation of the dead; and from the tenth to the fourteenth centuries cremation was common enough in the southeastern coastal provinces to create a timber shortage". In contrast, it is the current Communist government which "has made an immense effort to control erosion and reforest".[9] This activity, as he points out, "is no reflection of the traditional virtues of Taoism and Buddhism; on the contrary, it rests on their explicit (and, one might add, explicitly anthropocentric) denial".

Even those "primal" societies—like the Indians of North and South America, the Aboriginal people of Australia, or the Melanesian and Polynesian peoples of the Pacific—who are so often held up as examples of cultures where "the people lived in harmony with nature", and are sometimes seen as models for the creation of environmentally sound lifestyles, had a significant, and often negative, impact on their environment. The "nature" in which they lived was a nature which they had modified in quite significant ways — by for example, the regular burning of grasslands — and modified to suit their own, human, purposes. The extinction of the megafauna in America, for example, has often been associated with the arrival of humans on that continent. There have been suggestions that the practices of the Australian Aborigines contributed to the predominance of eucalypts and the relative sparsity of other species in the open forests of Australia, and there are probably few better examples of the consequences of ecological disaster than those which can be found in the sad history of Easter Island.

The truth would seem to be that rather than there being some direct correlation between the environmental impact of particular cultures and their underlying religious and ethical bases, there is, as Naess intimated, a far stronger connection with the extent of their economic and technological development. But even this is not a direct correlation. Societies which are essentially agriculturally based, like many of the African nations, have contributed substantially to the growth of the world's deserts, and many of the "pagan" and "animistic" tribes have been involved in the poaching of wild animals to the extent that many now face extinction. The rapidly developing societies of parts of Asia and South America are destroying rain forest at a prodigious rate, and the once "state-socialist" nations of the old Eastern Bloc have notorious levels of pollution. Ironically, it is those western nations, with their "Judeo-Christian ethos" and who have proceeded the furthest down the path to the development of a "technocratic-industrial" culture, where the growth of environmental movements has been strongest, and where their impact on governments and public policy has been of greatest significance.

Even if we cannot so readily attribute the "roots of our ecological crisis" to the predominance of a particular "anthropocentric" ethos within societies, might it not still make sense to promote an ecocentric or biocentric alternative as the basis on which we might develop the kind of culture necessary to deal with the consequences of that crisis? For isn't it more likely that a society where the majority of people share such an outlook would be more willing to "put the planet first", making the hard decisions which are necessary, than one where a narrow anthropocentrism reigns supreme? On this view, even if anthropocentrism cannot be identified as the cause of the problem, it might still be a barrier to its solution. If it is the case that "it is only in those political communities in which an ecocentric sensibility is widely shared that there will be a general consensus in favour of the kinds of far-reaching, substantive reforms that will protect biological diversity and life-support systems",[10] then there would be every reason to promote ecocentrism as a first step in the long and necessary process of re-construction. But while this modest version of deep ecology has some immediate appeal, there are difficulties with the approach.

While few would deny that significant *attitudinal* changes are necessary for the solution of our environmental problems, it is not nearly so clear that such changes can only be built on the kinds of sweeping *ethical* re-assessments that have been proposed by writers in this tradition. There are good reasons to suppose that not only are the kinds of ethical positions which have been put forward inadequate to the task they have been assigned, but that there are more powerful, and *politic*, alternatives available. We argue that rightly conceived a form of "Human Welfare Ecology"—Political Ecology—provides such an alternative. In order to make such a case, it is necessary to take a closer look at what is taken to be the basic error of such a position: its anthropocentrism.

Literally "anthropocentrism" means "human centredness", but this apparently straight-forward formulation can be understood in a variety of different ways. There are many different kinds and degrees of anthropocentrism.[11] However, in their "negative or critical task of dismantling anthropocentrism", deep ecological theorists have tended to lump these different meanings together, and often to present anthropocentrism in extreme forms. So Eckersley identifies the belief that "humans are the pinnacle of evolution and the sole locus of value and meaning in the world"[12] as the defining mark of an anthropocentric outlook. Aside from the way Eckersley's definition closes our eyes to the possibility of a less narcissistic humanism, what is important in this description is the combination of a particular understanding of humanity's place in *nature* with a particular *ethical* position. But it is clear that there is no necessary connection between these two different beliefs.

It is perfectly possible to accept that from a strictly evolutionary point of view we are simply "plain members of the biotic community"—that there are no "pinnacles" in the evolutionary schema—and yet to embrace an ethical position which does give special consideration to humans as the "locus of value and meaning in the world". We suggest that this particular combination of scientific understanding and ethical evaluation is the only reasonable response to the situation in which we find ourselves. Since the first of these views—that from the perspective of biological science humans do not have a central place—is relatively uncontroversial, it is the second—that humans have a central place in ethical consideration—which invites further examination. Can we, or should we, attempt to develop and promote a non-anthropocentric ethic as a primary means to the solution of our environmental problems?

The first thing to say is that it is not at all clear what such a non-anthropocentric ethic would actually involve, or what guidance it might give human behaviour. Even if we allow for the moment that it is logically possible to imagine a fully non-anthropocentric ethic, it is highly questionable whether such an ethic could provide clear guidelines for our actions towards the rest of the world, or to the extent it could, whether such guidelines would be at all appealing to people, particularly if *all* traces of anthropocentrism are removed. Take Naess' "central intuition" that "all organisms and entities in the ecosphere, as parts of the interrelated whole, are equal in intrinsic worth", or Warwick Fox's injunction that we should allow "all entities ... the freedom to unfold in their own way".[13] If we attempted to apply either of these views, *without qualification*, we could not act at all. If it is really true that *all* organisms are of *equal* worth, then there would be no basis on which I could place my individual needs (say, to eat a carrot or a parrot) above the needs of that organism "to grow and flourish". In satisfying my needs I have ignored the needs of another, equally worthy, organism. Given that, in order to survive, humans will have to do this many times in their lives, an impartial judge, working with such a biocentric ethic in mind, might well decide that the only ethical thing for humans to do is to commit immediate racial suicide. Unless we are willing to give ourselves *some* priority then—morally speaking—we cannot exist at all.

Both Naess and Fox avoid this kind of absurd conclusion, but only by adding qualifications which undermine the non-anthropocentric purity of their formulations. Naess introduces the notion of "vital (human) needs", while Fox adds the rider "within obvious kinds of practical limits". In both cases it is human interests or human needs which decide what is and is not vital, or obvious, or practical. As Tim Luke argues, a "soft anthropocentrism" lingers at the core of those "biocentric" or "ecocentric" positions which avoid the misanthropic madness of the unqualified stance.[14] This becomes even clearer in Fox's earlier attempt to defend biocentrism, where he argues that his position "does not entail the view that intrinsic value is spread evenly across the membership of the biotic community", but rather that "organisms are entitled to moral consideration commensurate with their degree of central organisation (or capacity for richness of experience)".[15] But this kind of view is perfectly compatible with anything but the most harshly narcissistic anthropocentrism: humans might not be the *only* valuable things, but they would certainly seem to be the *most* valuable.

A further line of defence for the plausibility of non-anthropocentrism can be found in Eckersley's insistence that "ecocentric theorists see each human individual and each human culture as just as entitled to live and blossom as any other species, *provided* they do so in a way that is sensitive to the needs of other human individuals, communities and cultures, and other life-forms generally".[16] While recognising that the flourishing of human individuals and groups "inevitably necessitates some killing of, suffering by, and interference with, the lives and habitats of other species", she suggests that in such cases we should "choose the course that will minimise such harm and maximise the opportunity of the widest range of organisms and communities—*including ourselves*—to flourish in their/our own way".[17] But this manoeuvre does not solve the problem precisely because there are very many instances where the attempt to *minimise* harm and *maximise* such opportunities would involve a great degree of suffering, and perhaps even the widescale elimination (however regrettably) of one particular species: humans.

If humans are only *included*, rather than given some kind of *priority*, in such moral and practical equations then it is difficult to see how a whole range of human activities could be continued with any kind of good conscience. Agriculture, for instance, even if conducted in a relatively environmentally benign way, could hardly be pursued under such a set of guidelines. This is because agriculture, in any of its forms, always involves the attempt to maximise the production of a particular and quite limited set of species, and this is necessarily to the detriment of a large number of species which might, otherwise, grow and flourish in the same area. The logic of the moral dilemma entailed for agriculture by the "inclusion without priority" approach is sharply focussed by Luke in a wilfully brutal example. He points out that it is a consequence of a biocentric ethic that "if one was caught in a spring brushfire ... (then one) ... would be bound ethically to save a California condor hatchling over a human child, because the former—given its rarity— is much more valuable".[18] There are those who would object to this example just because it is brutal and distasteful to contemplate, but for the defender of biocentric equality the problem is to see how such can, in the moral terms they allow, be condemned as brutal or distasteful. And, of course, these kinds of dilemmas constantly emerge in any attempt to apply a fully non-anthropocentric ethic:

> We might let great white sharks, like "Jaws", eat as many swimmers as he can find without fear of reprisal or allow grizzlies to chow down on campers and livestock as their mode of self-realisation. But, will we allow anthrax or cholera microbes to attain self-realisation in wiping out sheep herds or human kindergartens? Will we continue to deny salmonella or botulism micro-organisms their equal rights when we process the dead carcasses of animals and plants that we eat?[19]

The point is not so much that if taken literally these kinds of approaches give us no real solution to these kinds of dilemmas, it is that they generate these dilemmas in the first place. Thus they lead us in directions which have little, if any, connection with those broader humanistic and emancipatory concerns which writers like Eckersley, Naess and Fox are also concerned to defend.

However, these strong formulations of a non-anthropocentric ethic are, as we have seen, typically presented alongside much weaker accounts. Eckersley's position, for instance, is modified in substantially the same way as Fox's: "self-consciousness and capacity for richness of experience" are also taken to be relevant factors.[20] Eckersley goes on to suggest that "a nonanthropocentric perspective is one that ensures that the interests of nonhuman species and ecological communities ... are not ignored in human decision making *simply* because they are not human or because they are not of instrumental value to humans".[21] Again, this involves the shift away from the "inclusion without priority" stance: from a position which implies some kind of *equality* of consideration of the human and non-human to one where the only stipulation is that non-human interests should not be *ignored*. But again this does not entail a *non-anthropocentric* ethic, it is perfectly compatible with a soft (or even a quite firm) anthropocentrism.

This constant tendency of deep ecological reflections, to fluctuate between relatively pure expressions of non-anthropocentrism, and positions which allow a significant anthropocentric element arises from misunderstanding, or an unwillingness, however it might be motivated, to confront, the extent to which issues in this arena are essentially *human issues*. After all:

> these are inescapably human questions in the sense that they are questions for humans. This implies something further and perhaps weightier, that the answers must be human answers: they must be based on human values, values that human beings can make part of their lives and understand themselves as pursuing and respecting.[22]

This point is not a trivial confusion of the origins of a view and its content which Eckersley rightly dismisses. It is pointing to the fact that moral questions and answers must be ours if they are to be anything at all: that unless we find the question compelling, and unless the answer is livable, then there is no question and no answer. It is not that morality refuses to speak in such a case, but that morality lives only on the oxygen of humanity. Any ethic is a *human* construction, and even if it is formulated from the purest of motives, with no hint of self-interest, it cannot escape that heritage. Since an ecological ethic is about how humans should relate to their environment, it is inherently concerned with human choices, and how such choices are to be justified to other humans. We would not expect a wolverine, a shark or a swarm of soldier ants to follow such an ethic, and to do so would be futile. In suggesting that we can choose to act in wiser ways towards the rest of nature, and that we should do so, theorists in this tradition have already set us apart as "uniquely able, and therefore uniquely obliged". And it is not merely that we are "uniquely obliged",[23] for the deep ecologist it is surely *good* that we have, can realise and honour, such obligations. But then, on their own, they have identified a source of value in humanity which cannot be attributed to the biological world in general. To argue that humans should follow a particular set of moral rules in their dealings with the rest of nature is at once to place them in a special, and valuable, category, and one which (as far as we know) is occupied exclusively by humans. As the source of value, in this sense, humans have already been given a certain priority.

While it might be logically possible (although very odd) to deny that the ability to value, or to act ethically, are themselves valuable or ethically worthwhile, in the same way that it is possible to deny that the many other apparently unique characteristics of humanity are of any particular worth, to do so is to open the door to a whole variety of misanthropic programs. For all the attempted repudiation of the now notorious views that Ethiopians should "just be allowed to starve", and that the AIDS virus "was a welcome development in the necessary reduction of human population",[24] it should be recognised that such sentiments are perfectly *consistent* with a position which accords no special value to humans. Starvation and disease, after all, are perfectly natural phenomena, and the attempt to overcome them in other species (say, rabbits) could well be ecologically disastrous. Unless some element of anthropocentrism is allowed to our evaluations it is difficult to say *why* we should attempt to prevent starvation and disease in the human population; or, at the very least, what we might say to those who do find that conclusion congenial. The kind of "eco-fascism" described by Murray Bookchin might not be the necessary consequence of the acceptance of a totally non-anthropocentric ethic if only because such an ethic is empty, but to profess such views is to have no grounds upon which to oppose those with misanthropic intent.

To insist that humanity is a fundamental modality of moral concern is further implied by two key elements of moral life, both of which are misconstrued in deep ecology. The first mistake involves ignoring that essentially localising, and so anthropocentric, mechanism of moral understanding, *empathic identification.* While the second involves forgetting the localist foundations of the *reproduction* of moral life.

Beginning with the former it is surely true that we comprehend the nature and requirements of others as they bear on moral action and decision through our capacity to imaginatively place ourselves in their position. And it is equally true that to do this without falling into the projective fantasies of unbounded anthropomorphism or something even worse, we need the assurance of an underlying and substantial continuity between our own nature and that of the object of our moral concern. A certain localism of approach and understanding is then unavoidable. If the distance between our nature and that of the potential object of moral concern exceeds a certain point (and this point cannot be determined *a priori;* though for us today it certainly involves a certain neurophysiological similarity), then claims to empathic identification shade into pure fantasy.

It should not be thought that the emphasis we place on empathic identification in generating moral understanding cuts against the claim that humanity itself is a basic modality of moral concern. The apparent problem is that the claim that humanity is a fundamental modality of moral experience involves attributing moral standing to human beings who, because of their situation (eg. comatose or in other ways severely brain damaged), seem outside the range of possible empathic identification, and so outside the range of moral concern. In one sense, the *phenomenological* sense, this is true, if only because there may be nothing for the subject that it is like to be that subject, but in another, equally important sense, it is false, for we can empathise with their *position,* with their life. There is the thought—and the clearly non-fantastical thought—that "there, but for the grace of God, go I (or my children)" etc.

Further, to focus on empathy in this way is to insist that while humanity is a fundamental modality of moral concern, moral concern itself is not limited only to the human species, even if this concern crucially modulates about the possibility of a shared position, a shared possibility of life. In both the phenomenological and positional senses a case for a certain extra-human extension of moral concern naturally develops, though each extension involves too some diminution in the attainable degree of moral understanding, so in the stringency of moral obligation. In the phenomenological sense the basis of such extension rests on the degree of behavioural and physical similarities which hold between us and other creatures, while in the positional sense such extension rests upon an evolutionary understanding of our biological past. To ignore these possibilities is at best surprisingly obtuse, at worst a studied callousness. Here then we have the foundations of a "soft" anthropocentrism in which we see "the invariable allocation of greater value or preference ... to humans, while not however entirely excluding non-humans from moral consideration and claims".[25]

If, unlike the radical claims of biocentric moral equality, this "soft" anthropocentrism is compatible with a focal human welfarism, a further reason can be found if we look at the second essentially localising aspect to moral concern. So consider the unqualified deep ecological claim in terms of the following Tim Luke-style problem:

> You are walking along a jungle trail as it is approaching dusk. You round a bend and, in the failing light, see what is obviously a large animal violently attacking what is, equally obviously, a human being. Although the light is not good, you are an excellent shot, and have no doubt that you can hit what you aim for.[26]

What is to be done? For the adherent to biocentric equality one point is clear. It would not be right to unhesitatingly shoot the animal in order to save the human being. It may even be right to shoot the human being (imagine that they are old and decrepit, while the animal is vigorous, intelligent and endangered—a wolf perhaps). And here is the problem. *For what kind of people do we wish to have around us?* In particular—and assuming we are sane—what kind of moral sensibility will we prefer to inculcate in our fellows as they enter into the human world?

The question is far from trivial. It is an immediate consequence of the fact that the only reciprocal moral community we have (the community of mutually self-regulating moral agents) is our human moral community, and that this community itself exists at varying degrees of closeness and distance. Thus to the extent that morality determines acceptable and unacceptable paths of action and decision it cannot ignore such matters of proximity and distance. The point is familiar in a different context with traditional objections to act-utilitarianism. The principle of utility says only that we should maximise the amount of happiness in the world. Imagine then that those you are surrounded by are rigorous utilitarians. What kind of situation are you in? One thing to say is that it is a precarious situation, and in particular a situation in which such special obligations, as for example those involved in kin relationships and promising, are not reliable, and finally perhaps, not possible at all. We cannot, in this kind of situation, rely on others to keep their word, to treat us well, or to count the fact that one lives with them as imposing any limitations on what might and might not be done to us. If, as it seems to them, breaking their word to you, or indeed eliminating you from the world, will increase the amount of happiness in the universe, then that is their moral obligation, and that is the end of it.

Who would wish to live in such a world? And given that we construct the moral world by inculcating a moral sensibility in our children, who would educate their children to such a threatening sensibility? The answer surely is very few indeed. And the same holds equally for the kind of sensibility that would commit itself to the principle of biocentric equality. Here is a person whose moral seriousness involves undermining any reciprocity on which a worthwhile and secure life might depend. At the very least, and as the example shows, they are not the kind of person to take with one on safari; indeed they undermine the very possibility of such a mutual endeavour. Even more, the question "What kind of people do we wish to have about us?" has a certain force against strong anthropocentrism itself. For if we do not wish to surround ourselves with potential "ecopaths", nor do we generally want to have people around us who think it appropriate to treat any and all non-human creatures as mere objects. We may strike up various kinds of bonds with non-human beings besides the instrumental. We may value such beings for aesthetic reasons, we may find that empathy opens up areas of shared living and sets moral limits, and even the fact of ownership may assume a deep significance, beyond considerations of price. These bonds matter to us, they are real connections, real ties of obligation and sympathy, and we do not abandon them, or their importance, when we come to moral education. Ecopaths might be undesirable, but there is little more to be said for the incipient psychopath.

Morality must be something people find it worthwhile reproducing. At the very least this means it cannot assume the kind of undiscriminating impartiality the deep ecologist favours on pain of dissolving the bonds which give it meaning. More substantively, there is the fact that we typically owe more to those whose lives are deeply bound up with our own than we do to others at a greater distance. We may owe because some people have given us much more of the things we value, and we may also owe more just because we are a deep part of the life of another. It is on this point, and the importance it has for us as we initiate new members of the (our) moral world, that Kantian approaches to morality generally founder, and deep ecology is, ultimately, a variant on Kantianism in which the impartiality, and consequent insensitivity to the particular, goes beyond the bounds of Kant's otherwise admirable humanism.

The attempt to avoid the supposed biases of partiality comes out for orthodox Kantianism in the following example drawn from Bernard Williams.[27] One is standing on a beach alone, and there in the water in front of one are two people drowning, one a stranger, the other one's spouse. Conditions are such that it is apparent that one will only be able to make one rescue attempt. For the Kantian the appropriate decision-procedure is to curb one's initial ("biased") desire to save one's spouse, to step back, perhaps take out a coin, assign sides to the parties in the water, and flip it. Whichever side comes up determines without partiality (and so "justly") who is to be rescued.

Along with Williams we suggest that this is not the practice of someone who is morally admirable, and one way of putting the reason for this is to say that here there has been a thought *too many*. It should have been enough to determine action that it was one's spouse. But there has been the thought: why should *that* make any difference? And the case is fully congruent for deep ecology in the example introduced above. It should have been enough for the agent that it is a human being in mortal danger. There is something bloodless and inhuman about the further thought: why should the fact that a *human being* is threatened with a bloody death make any difference?

The theorists we have considered go to some lengths to avoid such "ecopathological" consequences, but their tactics typically involve them in a re-introduction of some form of anthropocentrism, albeit in a disguised form. An alternative tactic for the deep ecologist which also deserves mention, makes a similar attempt to overcome the problems of non-anthropocentrism, but through what amounts to a projection of human qualities onto the natural world. Lynn White Jnr., for example, looks to animistic religions as a basis for a new, and environmentally benign, ethic, but fails to realise this is to avoid anthropocentrism only by using anthropomorphism to subjugate nature. For animism, as Horton pointed out, involves an understanding of nature in human terms. The spirits and gods which pervade the world of animistic religions are essentially humans writ large if often distorted in various ways, who, through sacrifice, must be appeased, humoured and cajoled, in precisely the same way as humans who have power over us or can affect our lives in important ways. Animists do not so much understand humans through their independent understanding of nature, as explain the vagaries of the natural world by reference to their understanding of humans. A modern manifestation of the same process can be seen at work in the kind of interpretation of the "Gaia hypothesis" which is sometimes put forward by those who declare an attachment to a non-anthropocentric ethic.

What all of these points establish is that attempts to develop an ethic which removes any anthropocentric concern in our considerations of our relationships to the rest of the natural world are fundamentally mistaken. Not only would such an "ethic" deny us clear guides for human action, either to enhance the environment or to meet human needs, it would create new and tragic dilemmas. At least it would do so if it could present itself as an ethic for human beings, but this it cannot do without collapsing the distinction between the sane and the ecopathic.

This may seem a harsh judgement, but it is better to recognise the necessarily anthropocentric nature of human evaluations, and to work on this basis, than to try to promote an ethic among humans which denies themselves. On the other hand, it is equally clear that those who oppose such an ethic have typically construed it along the harshest lines. In fact, what they take to be the problem is not anthropocentrism as such, and certainly not our "soft" variety, but a particularly vicious or ill-informed form of anthropocentrism: one which is characterised not so much by its bias toward humanity as a limited, ignorant, and short-sighted greed of the kind that supports the misuse of the Principle of Least Disruption. It would be more enlightening to identify that limitation, ignorance and short-sightedness as the real problems, rather than focusing on the bogey of anthropocentrism.

Thus environmentalists can (and very often do) present a case for environmental protection in purely human-centred terms. One does not need to appreciate or value the non-human in order to recognise that humans, in virtually everything they do, are dependent upon the natural world. While there are many arguments upon which those concerned to defend the environment can draw, often the most forceful focus on the destructive effects of not doing so: if we destroy the environment we, ultimately, must destroy ourselves or our descendants. This, after all, follows directly from our understanding of ecology. We are animals, and like all other animals we depend on the ecosphere to provide us with the requirements for our continued existence. If we foul the source of all our benefits, then it is difficult to see in what sense we have gained for humanity. While there may be some immediate and short-term benefits to be gained for particular individuals by polluting waterways, pouring poisons into the air, or destroying tracts of forest, if these activities are carried on for long periods of time, and on a wide-scale, then they ultimately must affect us all in highly negative ways. To continue such activities, to be indifferent to the environment in that sense, is simply unreasonable from any humane viewpoint.

Arguably then, the environmental movement does not really *need* any more than this argument to begin making its case. And, if further reasons are required, there are a host of practical, economic, and essentially anthropocentric, arguments which can be brought into the dispute. There are good economic reasons for the preservation of wilderness, the prevention of pollution, and the husbanding of natural resources, when all costs are taken into account. If, for example, the long-term medical costs of high levels of pollution are added to the costs of manufacture, then the differential cost between highly polluting and non-polluting means of production takes on rather a different light. Equally, the potential economic costs of an accelerating "greenhouse effect", even if only the possible rises in sea levels are considered, are enormous.

Such an approach to environmental issues can quite easily pass Eckersley's "litmus ... issues [of] ... human population growth and wilderness preservation".[28] While these issues might not be *as* central to "human welfare ecology" as they purport to be on the "ecocentric" approach, there are a host of quite pragmatic reasons for the preservation of large areas of wilderness, and there is little doubt that there are significant portions of the globe where some reduction in human population would make a real contribution to the possibilities for the enhancement of the human quality of life, as well as to the preservation of environmental integrity. If it is the case that such arguments have not been taken as seriously as they should have been, then the culprit is not the anthropocentric outlook of our society, but our lack of understanding and foresight, and perhaps even our lack of that humanism deep ecologists decry, coupled with our apparent inability to create an economic system where the good of all (rather than just a few) is the basis for decision.

This is not meant as an argument in favour of a harshly anthropocentric view of nature. As we have seen, there are many degrees of anthropocentrism, and it is perfectly consistent with such a position to value non-human things and organisms, and to value them very highly. All that anthropocentrism requires is that the human is given some priority in the scale of values. It is perfectly consistent with an anthropocentric outlook to recognise that human life is intimately connected with the life of other organisms in the biosphere, to appreciate the beauty and wonder of that life, to empathise with it, and to value it for all its richness and diversity. It is even reasonable to suggest that anyone so alienated from nature that they do not see any value in the non-human leads an impoverished life. But to appreciate, even to love and revere, the natural is a perfectly human attitude, and one that does not require a "biocentric" approach, any more than to appreciate and value, say, a piece of finely crafted furniture, requires one to imbue it with the same intrinsic value that one might give to human beings. In fact one can use examples like this to argue that deep ecology typically misunderstands its real nature. Far from being a moral competitor to humanism, it may—at least in its "litmus" concern for "wild nature"—be better understood as a particular expression of human aesthetic sensibility, though such a reading diminishes any claims it might have to found a genuinely political program. Let us briefly sketch this aesthetic reading of deep ecology, for while as a moral movement it appears hopelessly flawed, understood as an aesthetic movement it may have something important to tell us, though in the end we think it tells us more about the nature of contemporary human society than about the natural world.

The first point to make is that the reconceptualisation we offer of deep ecology, while limited to the concern for wild nature, is not otherwise intended in a debunking spirit. On the contrary, the importance of the aesthetic in human life is not to be underestimated. Depending on the way one approaches this importance, it is a matter of avoiding the stultification of terminal boredom, or of ensuring the possibility of that creative imagination which makes meaning come alive. Consider the Platonic trilogy of the Good, the True, and the Beautiful, *sans* the latter. Without an aesthetic delight in discovering the nature of reality, the True becomes an uninteresting and lifeless body of propositions, useful, if at all, in a merely strategic or utilitarian sense, while morality or the Good uniformed by the aesthetic imagination, is an equally lifeless matter of discovering and upholding the determinations of an oppressively rigid "Duty". Certainly the individual or community which finds nothing of beauty in the world and their life in it, is in a pretty bad way. As we shall see, it is one of the results of viewing deep ecology as an aesthetic movement that we can interpret it as a protest against the loss of a sense of beauty in things of the human world. Our aesthetic imagination, for the deep ecologist, finds no succour at the breast of our anthropocentric lives and concerns, and so is driven to escape (or retreat) to the non-anthropocentric world of the "natural".

Deep ecologists insist, as we have seen, that we require a "new ecological ethic", an ethic distinguished from our previous ethics in being, in the relevant sense, non-anthropocentric. But before leaping to the conclusion that this is a moral ethic, we should appreciate that the essential point is the call for a *non-anthropocentric mode of access to the world that founds reasons for acting which embody a respect for the integrity of natural objects*. It is of no use simply to abandon the human point of view, nor to try to extend it to include everything in the world—either way, that will mean to have no view at all. But this is not something deep ecologists should take themselves to be committed to. Rather the point is to establish the possibility of a human point of view—a view of the world possible to creatures like us—which does not place anything *objectionably* human at the centre of concern.

Robyn Eckersley makes a distinction between *formal* and *substantial* anthropocentrism which is useful here. Formal anthropocentrism, she says, simply reflects the point that whatever vision of the world deep ecologists come up with, it must be a point of view that human beings can utilise. Substantial anthropocentrism, which she rejects, involves this vision being structured in some way so as to further specifically human ends and goals. As we have seen, this distinction, while essential to deep ecology, cannot be sustained if we insist that we are developing a new moral ethic. But there is a far more persuasive case to be made for the validity of the distinction in the context of aesthetics. Aesthetics, like morality, like anything human beings do, is formally anthropocentric, but there are reasons to think it less objectionably local in nature than morality.

The crucial point is that in aesthetic experience, unlike moral experience, (at least on the everyday understanding of the two), the object of the experience makes no *direct demands for action* on the spectator. The object is not viewed in such a way that it generates demands which bear directly on our will, leading us at once (if not finally) to favour certain kinds of actions towards it over others, and nor does it engender in us any system of desires for doing anything immediately with it, except perhaps (and this only indirectly, through the power of the object as it exercises itself in our experience) to continue gazing at it, or listening to it, or whatever. Indeed, if we look at some object and see it immediately through the eyes of desire or duty, then we are not contemplating for the moment anything aesthetic, for it is the mark of aesthetic experience that in it the will is *silent*. It is a different matter for morality— there the will is not silent, but actively called by the object to fulfil certain demands. With the will involved in this immediate fashion it follows that moral demands must be suited to key directly into our standing motivational possibilities as human beings, and, of course, these possibilities are not endless, but are constrained by the contingencies of our nature and existence. But it is not at all obvious that a mode of appreciation of objects, like the aesthetic, in which the will is silent and does not (pre)determine the interest we take in that which we confront, must be limited in this way, constrained by prudence to the grosser demand of human life, or by morality to the homocentric demands of empathetic identification.

Consider how the will is engaged in moral experience. It is called forth to answer the demands of the object, in particular, to respect its needs, desires and interests, and that means first identifying these states. This identification is empathic and so made on analogy with our own case. We "put ourselves in the shoes of others", and, from there, decide on the interests, etc., of the object. But "putting ourselves in the shoes of another", constrained by the requirement of relevant explanatory similarity, simply indicates the essentially anthropocentric focus of moral experience. With aesthetic experience, on the other hand, in its silence to the demands of the will, there is no need for this kind of empathic identification to constrain the possibilities of identification. True, the aesthetic understanding in question will be the aesthetic understanding of a human being, living in a certain society, and answerable to that society's traditions of aesthetic understanding (something true of all our sensitivities to the world, independently of that to the most brutal natural facts), but the claim of substantial anthropocentrism is severely compromised by the independence the experience has of the will and of the analogical demands of identification.

If the aesthetic reading can make more sense of the non-anthropocentric aspiration of deep ecology, it may seem that it does so at the expense of eliminating that which is most important to deep ecologists. For aesthetic experience, as we have insisted, involves the silence of the will. But what policies and strategies for the environment would, or could, follow from a mode of vision that, by itself, does not motivate us in these ways?

The first point to make is that in one sense this absence of motivation is just what deep ecologists want, for one thing the aesthetic mode of vision does do is to entirely rule out the appropriateness of *instrumental* attitudes in this area. It may be thought that the same is true of moral vision—that it rules out instrumental considerations entirely—but this would be a mistake. For while to view an object aesthetically is to view it in a way that rules out our holding and acting on instrumental attitudes towards it, to view another morally is not at all to see them in a way which simply rules out instrumental thought. Rather it rules out instrumental thought which fails to acknowledge that underneath the taxi-driver, or dentist, or politician, or warden of the university, or whoever, there is, there remains, a centre of moral standing. Morality rules out pure instrumentalism and insists on humanity and decency in our dealings with each other, but peak aesthetic experiences seem to rule out even this decent instrumentalism. You cannot see, say, *Blue Poles* as an aesthetic object and, at the same time, as just the thing to cover that bare space on the wall at home, nor even do so in a "decent" fashion, perhaps by paying a "fair price" for the service.

If instrumentalism is ruled out in the having of aesthetic experiences, and if many of those objects deep ecologists wish to value cannot be approached through empathic identification and so cannot generate direct moral demands on the will, then it may seem that the aesthetic approach is motivationally vacuous; but that would be a mistake. For while the will is silent *in* aesthetic experience, it most assuredly is not silent *about* such experiences. It is no accident that we build galleries and museums to house works of aesthetic value, even though the thought that this is where such things should be housed is no part of the aesthetic experience itself. It is *important* to us that the will is—can be—silent in aesthetic experience, and all this is formally anthropocentric. But it is not substantially anthropocentric, for the possibility of aesthetic experience means that it is important to us that there are objects which are suited to, or can sustain, this experience. And these are objects which we must be able to experience and think of independently of the human-centred moral demand for sympathy, or of our equally human-centred instrumental purposes. The very point of the aesthetic attitude on this view is to protect and to cherish that which makes no human, no moral and no instrumental, demands on us.

Aesthetic experience, and so aesthetic value, depends on the possibility of attending to an object in all its particularity, and without instrumental or moral thoughts intruding. This does not mean that the objects of aesthetic appreciation might not themselves constitute a causal or moral danger to the individual or community, it means only that there are times when they can be viewed, can be attended to, without these concerns intruding. Both natural items and non-natural, humanly produced, items, have, in the past, been able to sustain this kind of attention. Sunsets and Modigliani's have both been able to sustain such reverential experiences. The trouble today is that increasingly, humanly produced objects, and particularly, but not only, those produced as "aesthetic objects", are unsuited, or unable, to sustain this kind of attention, to provide us this kind of relaxation in and with the world.

Increasingly, it seems to us, our world is *saturated* with the now all-too-human. It is saturated both with instrumental reasoning, as members of the Frankfurt School have endlessly insisted, and, as the media continually bring the details of an often terrible and ravaged human world to us, with moral demands which are far in excess of our powers of response, even comprehension. The human world today leaves little time, less and less all the time, for the kind of detached, willess, absorption in an object which drives away boredom and enables us to create and invigorate the meaning in our lives. Our historical position is such that, for many of us, anything human is simply unsuited, too full of desire or moral demand, for the kind of attention which recognises the aesthetic value of the world. There is, so it often seems, nowhere else for our aesthetic sense to go but away from, even out of, the human world and to the world instead of wild nature. It is here, outside the constraints of desire and morality, that we overcome the boredom of a saturated life, and here in wild nature that the meaning in and of our lives can be (re)discovered.

If this is so then deep ecology is both a protest against the condition of the human world—against the terrifying boredom and meaninglessness of a world in which everything is to be used, or in which we are continually subject to impossible moral demands on our time and kindness—and an affirmation of the importance of the aesthetic in human lives. It may not be a moral position in opposition to humanism as many of its proponents contend, nor does its insistence on leaving certain parts of the natural world alone constitute anything like a complete politics, but, on the appropriate terms, it deserves to be taken very seriously.

However it is for the aesthetic interpretation of deep ecology, what is important is that the case for the preservation of the environment does not, ultimately, depend on a particular, and particularly pure, even impossible, view of our ethical obligations to the natural world. If it did then we could only conclude that the green position rested on empty air. While there will always be some people who profess a selfless devotion to nature, it is unlikely that this attitude would pervade the whole of society, nor is the possibility a particularly pleasant one.

Currently, the major opposition to environmental reform comes from groups who stress the benefits of unregulated economic development for the community. To focus on the human benefits, material and moral, to be gained from improvements to the environment is to meet such arguments on their own grounds and ultimately to undermine them. Arguments which focus on the "standard of living", for example, can be countered by references to the "quality of life". A narrowly economistic concern with human welfare might be the starting point for many, but it can hardly be the end of the story for any of us. Once we recognise that human communities always exist within broader ecological communities, and that the welfare of those communities are intimately connected to each other, then the way forward might be a little clearer. What is immediately apparent from our experience of environmental degradation is that a longer-term perspective in human affairs is required. In so many cases, short-term economic and other gains have been pursued at the expense of long-term environmental losses, and losses which ultimately might prove to over-shadow such gains: the search for one kind of welfare has endangered another. If today we claim to be humanists, it is equally true we have a bad conscience about our relation to those yet to come, or whose going will be long after ours. Often we use our economistic obsessions to hide, even rationalise, this uncomfortable selfishness. It is in its recognition of the overwhelming importance of such long-term considerations in the search for a better life that the green movement presents such a fundamental challenge to existing political and economic beliefs and programs. But if that challenge loses its sense that the primary aim is still *human* welfare then it also loses much of its force.

Notes

1   Lyn White Jnr., "The Historic Roots of the Ecological Crisis", in J. Barr (ed.), *The Environmental Handbook*, (London: Ballantine/Friends of the Earth, 1971), pp. 3-16. The following quotations are from this article.
2   Arne Naess, "The Shallow and the Deep, Long-Range Ecology Movement", *Inquiry*, 16.
3   William Grey, "Anthropocentrism and Deep Ecology", *Australasian Journal of Philosophy*, 1993, Vol. 71, No.4, p. 463.
4   M. Bookchin, "Social Ecology Versus Deep Ecology", *Socialist Review*, 1988, 18 (3), p. 18. The following quatations are from this article.
5   W. Fox, "The Deep Ecology-Ecofeminism Debate and its Parallels", *Environmental Ethics*, 1989, Vol. 11 (Spring), p. 16
6   Robyn Eckersley, *Environmentalism and Political Theory*, (London: UCL Press, 1994). The following quotations all come from this work.
7   See for example, Robin Horton, in M. Hollis & S. Lukes, (eds.), *Rationality and Relativism*, (Oxford: Basil Blackwell, 1983).
8   Yi-Fu Tuan, "Our Treatment of the Environment in Ideal and Actuality", *American Scientist*, 1970, p. 244.
9   *Ibid.*, p. 248. Though it is to be pointed out that much of this effort has now been abandoned in the quest for rapid economic growth.
10   Eckersley, *op. cit.*, p. 185.
11   Fox, *op. cit.*, 1989, p. 13.
12   Eckersley, *op. cit.*, p. 28.
13   Fox, *op. cit.*, p. 6.
14   Tim Luke, "The Dreams of Deep Ecology", *Telos*, 1988, No. 76, Summer, pp. 81-83.
15   Fox, *op. cit.*, pp. 199-200.
16   Eckersley, *op, cit.*, p. 56.
17   *Ibid.*, p. 57.
18   Luke, *op. cit.*, p. 87.

19   *Ibid.*, p. 82.
20   Eckersley, *op. cit.*, p. 57.
21   *Ibid.*
22   Bernard Williams, "Must a Concern for the Environment be Centred on Human Beings?", in Taylor, C.C.W., ed., *Ethics and the Environment*, (Corpus Christi College, Oxford, 1992).
23   *Ibid.*, p. 65.
24   Although for a kind of defence of these views from the perspective of "deep ecology" see: K. Sale, "Deep Ecology and its Critics", *The Nation*, May 14, 1988, p. 675.
25   Richard Routley and Val Routley, "Against the inevitability of human chauvinism" in K.E. Goodpaster and K.M. Sayer (eds), *Ethics and Problems of the Twenty-First Century*, (Notredame: University of Notredame Press, 1979), p. 47.
26   The example and its implications for deep ecology are discussed in more detail in Tony Lynch and David Wells, "Non-Anthropocentrism?: a Killing Objection", *Environmental Values*, 1998, Vol. 7, pp. 151-163.
27   Bernard Williams, "Persons, Character and Morality", in his *Moral Luck*, (Cambridge: Cambridge University Press, 1981), pp. 1-19.
28   Eckersley, *op. cit.,* p. 29.

3 Green Politics and the Question of Growth

One of the most common claims of environmentalists is that their views represent a new direction in social and economic thought. While this claim is often based on the kinds of ethical stances which we have already discussed, it is also common to identify the issue of growth—and particularly of economic growth—as a central point of diversion from more traditional modes of thought. So, there is the assertion that "Green Politics is neither Right nor Left but Ahead", and the reason usually cited for this apparent transcendence of the political spectrum is its attitude to growth. Where both Right and Left have, either implicitly or explicitly, relied upon continual economic growth to solve a variety of social and political problems, environmentalists tend to reject this approach as untenable in the long term. Jonathon Porritt, for example, suggests that "an increase in Gross Domestic Product (GDP) *inevitably* means an increase in Gross National Pollution".[1] This represents a major challenge to the dominant ideology of much of the world, where economic growth is often presented as a panacea to virtually all the ills which bedevil society.

What such an approach to economics offers the population is the promise of a steadily increasing "standard of living". This is a powerful promise, and one which has, generally, been accepted by people all over the world. To oppose it is difficult, unless some equally powerful alternative can be provided. In this case that alternative comes in the form of the notion of the "quality of life". And even to present this as an alternative is of real significance, primarily because it had always been assumed that to increase the "standard of living" was also to improve the "quality of life". To present these as different, even incompatible goals, is to strike at the heart of the basic rationale of the economic programs of most societies. And those with an ecological bent, along with some allies in this cause, have developed a range of arguments which, even if they may not be totally devastating, at least take some gloss off the kinds of argument for growth at any cost which have been the basis for so much of public policy and political decision.

These arguments operate at a number of levels but they tend to focus upon the way in which "standards of living" have usually been measured. Typically when comparing the "standard of living" of various countries the measure used by economists is the Gross Domestic Product (GDP) per capita: the economic output (in monetary terms) of a society is divided by the population to produce a figure which is taken to have some direct connection with the living standards enjoyed by the people. However, while this kind of measure has the virtue of precision, in the sense that it is possible to arrive at hard and fast figures, it is also obviously inadequate—even if it is only taken as a direct indication of the levels of material well-being which exist in a particular society. That is, even apart from any consideration of non-material values GDP per capita does not provide a clear basis for the judgement of "standards of living". It is, in fact, inadequate—even in its own terms—for a variety of reasons.

Most importantly, GDP only provides us with a measure of the extent of economic activity as considered in monetary terms. It has nothing to say about the nature of that activity, and does not record anything which does not involve financial transactions. Take, for example, the case of packaging. In some instances at least, it is quite clear that the packaging of various products is far in excess of the requirements necessary to protect the product: it has far more to do with marketing than with preserving the goods against damage or deterioration. Yet, if such a product is successful in the market, the value of the packaging itself, the cost of collecting it as rubbish, and perhaps even the cost of re-cycling it, will all be considered as contributions to economic growth which increases GDP. In such a case the "standard of living", calculated in economic terms, has been "improved", but it would be very difficult to point to any way in which people's lives have actually been enhanced. Indeed, it would be reasonable to argue that, in any overall system of accounting, the "quality of life" has actually deteriorated. The production and distribution of the packaging will almost certainly have contributed to air or water pollution in one way or another, and there will have been some loss in the basic resources used to manufacture the material. While it is true that some individuals or companies might have profited, and some personal "standards of living" may have risen, it is clear that no positive contribution has been made to the general well-being of society, and yet this is what GDP is supposed to measure.

Nor is this an isolated example. It is not difficult to think of a whole range of activities which involve some form of economic production, which contribute little or nothing to any genuine increase in the "standard of living" and which may actually decrease it, but which are recorded as increases in

GDP. At the most extreme, for example, a high incidence of car accidents will be seen as a contribution to economic growth: not only will greater production be involved in the replacement and repair of damaged vehicles, but the costs of police activity, ambulances, hospitals, and even funeral parlours will all be recorded as increases in "production". And, if things are considered on a global scale, then the vast resources which are directed towards military purposes will be seen as "improving" standards of living, even though the result of actually using these resources is essentially destructive. There are, quite simply, many ways in which the statistical measures of production are increased, while no real benefit accrues to the population.

Equally, it is not just that the measure of GDP includes things which most of us might consider as having either no positive, or perhaps even a negative effect on our lives, but that even to the extent it does measure apparent contributions to our material well-being, it makes no distinction between the real worth of these contributions. All it measures, and all it can measure, is the extent of economic activity, as recorded in monetary terms, not the nature of that activity. In terms of the measurement of GDP the production of executive toys is seen as just as great a contribution to a society's "standard of living" as an equivalently valued production of food for the undernourished. In such terms the production of a luxurious hotel is as important as a hospital, or an expensive power-cruiser, which might be used very infrequently, as a number of houses for the homeless. It is for this reason that comparisons between the "standards of living" of peoples in various countries often seem so odd. It is not unusual, for instance, for people from countries with relatively modest "standards of living" to be horrified at the costs of such basic items as food, clothes and housing in societies with, apparently, much higher "standards of living". At its most obvious, a small increase in GDP brought about by improved agricultural production in a society where many are starving might well have a far greater impact on real "standards of living" than an equivalent rise in an already wealthy society. So, it is not only that increases in GDP per capita might bring no real improvement to people's lives, but that even when, on average, we might be able to point to some "improvements", the *extent* of that improvement—particularly if the total population is taken into account—may have very little connection to the apparent rise in GDP per capita.

At the same time, the fact that GDP per capita is an *average* measure means that it may tell us very little about what is happening to the majority of people in a particular society. For what is really important, as Stephen Jay Gould has pointed out in another context, is not averages but distributions. It is perfectly possible for the average wealth of a society to increase substantially, and yet have a situation where most people are actually worse off in real terms.[2] In his "infamous" calculation the MIT economist Paul Krugman shows how this can happen.[3] His figures indicate that, over the last twenty years, something like 70% of all the extra income generated in the USA has been accumulated by less than 1% of the population while, at the same time, real wages for the bottom 80% of wage earners appear to have declined by roughly 1% per year. Thus while wealth and income per capita have risen substantially on *average*, their *distribution* has become less and less equal. The benefits of a growing GDP in such cases, and even where only economic considerations are taken into account, means little to the great majority of people. While the average "standard of living" has risen, for most people it has declined.

The inadequacy of economic measures like GDP as indicators of the real quality of people's lives does not only arise from the way in which production is measured, counted and distributed, what is of equal significance is what is left out of the equation. Even in seemingly material and economic terms there are many human activities which are highly productive but which simply do not appear in the records of economic statisticians. So, for example, consider the case of a family which grows its own vegetables and raises chickens. If this family uses this home-grown food to create a meal then, in terms of GDP, absolutely nothing has happened. If, in contrast, they buy the food to prepare the same meal, then GDP has been increased by the cost of that food. If the family goes to a restaurant and buys the same meal then GDP has been increased even further, and if they go to a very expensive restaurant then the increase is even more significant. Yet, in all these cases, the same thing has happened: a family has been fed. In fact, there are a host of activities which we undertake in our homes or in cooperation with our friends and neighbours which do not involve any monetary exchange and, therefore, in terms of GDP simply do not exist. Yet they may be very important, even vital, to our lives and well-being. It is bewildering to discover that if we had paid someone to perform these activities (assuming we could afford to) then we would have contributed to increasing the "standard of living" of the nation, but if we do them ourselves they achieve nothing—at least in economic terms.

It is also clear that this hidden "household" or "neighbourhood" economy is not just a minor element in economic production which has simply been overlooked, and is not really that important. For a significant proportion of humanity it is the very basis of their existence. Anyone who considers the economic statistics of the poorer countries in the world with "standards of living" in mind must soon recognise this. The average family incomes in many of these societies would not be sufficient to support a family in one of the wealthier societies for more than a few weeks, and yet they continue to survive. The reason they are able to do this is that so much of the "economy" that supports them has absolutely no impact on economic statistics because it involves no financial exchanges. The production of food, clothing or shelter for personal or communal use, or even for barter, is simply not considered as "production" for the purposes of calculating GDP. In fact, before the extension of the western monetary economy to virtually all corners of the world there were many societies where GDP—as we calculate it—was virtually nil. We could only conclude that such societies had *no* "standard of living". And yet at least some of these societies had aspects of their "quality of life" which we might well envy.

In such societies the informal "economy" was virtually 100% of the overall economy, but even in more "developed" nations the contribution this kind of activity makes to our lives is far from negligible. Hugh Stretton, for example, has calculated that if the real value of this kind of economy were taken into account, then it would make up somewhere over 30% of the value of all economic activity.[4] With a possible margin of error of this magnitude there is every reason to look on more traditional accounts of the "standard of living" with a great deal of scepticism. And even such estimates only tell a little of the story. If we are concerned with the real "quality" of our lives rather than notional "standards of living", then we need to recognise that there is a degree of satisfaction which can be gained from such activities as gardening, renovating houses, caring for our children, or involving ourselves in community projects, which gives them a value much greater than their apparent economic cost. We can calculate the "value" of child-minding, for instance, by reference to the commercial rates which apply, but there are few of us who would believe that this is a fair assessment of what we gain. Even more, there is a sense in which what is largely produced in households and neighbourhoods is the most important product of all, but the value of that product is never recorded in any (even non-traditional) statistics. How, after all, are we to place an economic value on *people*?

And it is not just that such standard economic measures tend to overlook or ignore many of the things which are highly significant in our lives, but that they also tend to take little or no account of many of the negative social, cultural and environmental effects which are often associated with economic growth. So, for example, the elevated levels of crime and violence which are characteristic of so many of the larger urban centres in the world seem to bear at least some connection with the development of an increasingly economically oriented culture. In a world where affluence is highly visible, where the material indicators of status abound, where measures of individual worth are more and more made in monetary terms, where the values of conspicuous consumption pervade society, and yet where many have little chance of attaining the accoutrements of affluence or, if they do, find them less than satisfying, then it is not surprising to discover the kind of dislocation that leads to a variety of anti-social activities. While it is true that this is not a hard and fast connection, it is equally true that such a trend has occurred in many societies. What is important is not so much the causality of this process, but the fact that this kind of change is simply not considered when "standards of living" are measured. If anything, these trends have bolstered the growth of the "security industry" and, thereby, actually increased GDP.

One way of justifying this would be to point out that as people become more affluent they are able to buy more security, and in that sense they have gained. In terms of standard economic measurements this makes perfect sense: people seemingly have more of something—security services—so they are better off. In fact, the growth of the "security industry" presupposes (and, if merely through its heightened visibility, encourages) the growth in the community of a sense of *insecurity*. The product that is bought—security services—can never finally satisfy the consumers' desire for it, and for just those reasons which led to its being offered and desired in the first place. Here the market plays a cruel joke on us, though the joke and its cruelties are not merely unregistered in the GDP, but appear as an increase in the "standard of living" and so are taken to indicate an increase in our levels of well-being, rather than the absolute reduction it really is.

An even more obvious example can be seen in the case of the so-called "diseases of affluence". An increasing proportion of medical problems in the wealthy societies are directly connected with the kinds of lifestyles which affluence allows. This, in turn, has led to increased expenditure in the relevant medical areas, expenditure which is recorded as a significant contribution to economic growth. What GDP records is the monetary solutions to a problem, it takes no account of the causes or background to those problems. Yet it is clear, in terms of any notion of the real "quality of life" that something has been lost rather than gained. GDP provides a measure of certain kinds of benefits which people gain, but in a great many cases it takes little or no account of the losses involved. And it is in the area of the environment that this disjunction between apparent economic gains and real and significant losses is often drawn into its sharpest focus.

As we will suggest in later chapters, environmental goods are often treated as common goods in society, and because such common goods belong to everyone in general, and no one in particular, their significance is seriously undervalued (even though they are basic to all economic production). This is because the profits which might accrue from the exploitation of such resources are gained by individuals and organisations and can be easily measured by normal accounting procedures. The costs associated with their destruction or degradation, on the other hand, are spread throughout the whole community in a way which does not appear on any individual balance sheet. Because they are spread so widely, even the direct economic costs of such activities are extremely difficult to pin down, and some of them will even appear as examples of increased economic activity. So, for example, the indiscriminate logging of water-sheds might well lead to soil erosion, leading to the siltation of rivers and increased flooding. In such a case not only will the profits of the foresters be recorded as a positive gain in terms of economic activity, the measures taken by landholders or communities to prevent erosion or control flooding will also be seen as productive activities, and recorded as additions to capital. In many such cases the process of environmental degradation, particularly when it attracts some human activity aimed at its amelioration, is regarded as an addition to economic activity rather than as a cost to the community, even though any overall consideration of gains and losses might well lead to the conclusion that the costs are much higher than the benefits.

In a strict economic sense many of these common resources—the air, the water, the minerals in the soil, and the organic life which is sustained by these—are considered to have absolutely no value in their own right. In the logic of free market economics they are treated as free goods, to be taken and used at will. It is only when they are subject to human use and that use involves some monetary exchange, that they acquire any economic worth. Thus the price of minerals in the market (assuming there is adequate production to meet demand) will largely be determined by the cost of the extraction and transport of those minerals, there is no component in the equation which attributes any value to the minerals themselves. Even when scarcity becomes a factor, so that prices rise well beyond the costs of exploitation, the additional amount is recorded as pure profit in the accounts of the organisation involved. Except for the artificial levies imposed by governments, there is no point at which the actual minerals are regarded as having a cost. And this is the case with a whole range of environmental goods: the cost of fish is the cost of catching them; of timber the cost of felling and milling trees; of water the cost of storage and transport, and so on. This is not because these things do not have any real value, only that their value is diffuse. This cost is spread among the community as a whole and never recorded, even though the community ultimately must pay through the loss of forests, declines in air and water quality, and the increasing scarcity of resources.

In fact it is just because there *is* a limited recognition of the communal ownership of environmental goods that governments can and have justified regulation of their use. But even to the very limited extent that governments have applied conditions and charges to the use of these resources they have typically been caught in a double bind in terms of their economic measures of "standards of living". This is because to control their use seems, at least at first glance, to undermine the potential for economic growth and development. So, for example, if a particular industry creates significant amounts of air or water pollution then to enforce the installation of anti-pollution devices is to reduce economic efficiency and productivity: a greater capital input would be required for a given amount of production. To regulate fisheries also has the same effect: to the extent that fishing fleets are not used to their full potential, productive capital remains idle. To leave exploitable minerals in the ground or harvestable timber in national parks is to close avenues for investment which might substantially improve GDP. In every case the search for economic growth, it would seem, could only be aided by the total deregulation of such industries, and even the problems this would create might well open avenues for new enterprises and new developments, increasing economic activity in areas like water purification, recycling, cleaning, materials substitution, or intensive agriculture. However, what somebody imbued with a pure "economic" world-view would unhesitatingly identify as "progress", an "ecological" thinker might rightly see as disaster.

At its most basic level such an approach to the creation of higher "standards of living" may be disastrous because it is simply not sustainable. In the name of economic growth such an approach undermines not only the quality of life, but the viability of much of economic activity itself. While common goods may be treated as "free" goods for the purposes of economic accounting, they are not truly free and they are not infinite. Moreover, because such common goods are the basic elements in all forms of production, to treat them as if they were free, using them in increasingly wasteful ways, is to create the conditions for rapid economic decline. As resources become scarcer, and as the problems of pollution begin to affect the oceans, the forests and the soil, overall productivity must be affected in negative ways. The exploitation of mineral deposits comes to require greater inputs of capital and time as increasingly marginal deposits are developed. Stocks of marine animals and fish experience decline and become increasingly difficult (and more expensive) to catch. Agriculture comes to require greater inputs if yields are to be maintained, and forests, diminished by the effects of acid rain and over-exploitation, increasingly struggle to meet demand. At the same time, the kind of health and other problems associated with an increasingly polluted environment inevitably require a greater share of the economic cake. And so living standards (however they are calculated) are substantially reduced, while the "quality of life" enjoyed by the inhabitants of such a reduced world is affected in even more significant ways. The problem with GDP in this area is that while it measures economic activity in the short-term, it takes no account of the long-term costs associated with current developments. It records the exploitation of mineral deposits, but not the long-term costs of substitution when those minerals becomes scarce; the profits to be gained from the destruction of forests, but not the costs of re-afforestation; the productivity of agriculture, but not the costs of erosion control; the use of air and water to dispose of waste, but not the losses associated with pollution. In these ways it can give a very false picture of what is actually happening in people's lives.

Given such an array of arguments, it is not surprising to discover that many who have taken on an "ecological" world-view have called for zero, or even negative, economic growth. While they can provide no comparably clear measure of "quality of life", the problems they identify in the relationship between economic growth (or, at least, its measurement) and apparent rises in the "standard of living", are sufficient to regard raw economic growth itself with a good deal of suspicion. Measurements like GDP, as they suggest, give no indication of the real value of economic activity. They say little about how wealth is distributed and often record things with a negative impact on human life as economic gains. They ignore much human activity which creates real benefits and just as much which is destructive, and they take little account of the long term environmental (and, therefore, ultimately human) costs of economic activity. The statistics applauded as indicators of economic success are often much better indicators of long-term declines in the real quality of people's lives. Moreover, from an "ecological" viewpoint, the fundamental assumptions of the proponents of economic growth are dangerously at odds with the realities of the world.

In particular, what appears to be missing from the arguments for continuing, and continuous economic growth is any sense of limitations—of the finite character of the world. In recording, analysing and applauding the growth of industrial civilisation economists typically have taken what is, and what *must be*, an aberrant situation as the norm. Because they have focused on a period of exponential growth in human history, they have not only ignored the much longer periods of time when relative stability was the norm, but have forgotten the essential impossibility of continual growth in a finite environment. If it is true, as seems likely, that a number of those finite limitations are now appearing on the immediate horizon, then the vision of continued growth and progress which they promote is little more than a dangerous sham. It is a sham because it cannot be achieved, and it is dangerous because the attempt to achieve it might well be so destructive that any new balance of nature could well be at a level which is grim indeed. Far better, it would seem, to recognise those limitations and to work within them, to concentrate on the "quality of life", rather than on a flawed notion of the "standard of living"—a notion which has not really produced what it promised in any case.

However, while these arguments are powerful, and while they do indicate some of the great weaknesses of the current concentration on economic growth at almost any cost, it is not nearly so clear that the degree of antagonism to the vision of economic progress expressed by many "ecological" theorists is really an appropriate response. Such thinkers and writers may have identified some of the major flaws in "economic" visions, displaying the partial character of their understandings of the workings of the world, but all too often their own visions and programs are not without serious problems. In rejecting a simplistic "economic" approach to life it is tempting to replace it with an equally simplistic "ecological" viewpoint. This is particularly obvious (as it always is) at the level of sloganeering. Calls for "zero economic growth" or "negative industrial growth" clearly fall into this category. While they may appear to follow from the conclusions of the "ecological" critique of "economic" thinking, they do not really do so, and the fact that they can be presented as serious alternatives to the visions of growth and progress which still predominate in most societies, indicates a fundamental weakness in some "ecological" understandings.

While environmentalists and others have developed an impressive critique of the "growth mentality", expressed as an unreflective search for economic growth at virtually any cost, this critique does not really lead to the kind of conclusions some of them wish to draw. What this critique suggests is that measures like GDP are so seriously flawed that they give an entirely false impression of the benefits of economic growth, but this does *not* mean that economic growth, even as measured by GDP, is always destructive of the environment, or that a policy of zero or negative growth would provide any effective solution to our environmental problems, or even that economic growth has no positive contribution to make to the real quality of our lives. However, because the antagonism to economic growth has become so entrenched within at least some elements of the green movement, these points need to be explored in more detail.

As a beginning it is only necessary to point out that, in precisely the same way that it is possible to give examples of growth in GDP which are environmentally damaging and which do undermine the quality of life, it is equally possible to provide examples which indicate otherwise. It seems clear, for example, that the increasing concern with environmental issues itself opens up possibilities for the development of industries and activities which might contribute substantially to economic growth, and yet whose overall effects are largely beneficial to the environment. The re-afforestation of large areas of marginalised agricultural land provides a perfect illustration. While it is true that the initial removal of such areas from agricultural use would entail some loss in overall productive capacity, the loss would not be great. When all the inputs required to produce from such areas are considered their economic productivity is often very low. It is for this reason that so many farmers have found it so difficult to maintain their properties as viable economic units. Furthermore, even initially, the increased production of nurseries, and the activity of planting and maintaining the areas themselves would contribute to economic activity, while in the long-term the economic benefits could be substantial. Properly managed forest areas, after all, can be highly productive. They can provide not only firewood for heating and timber for building but, if planted with this purpose in mind, a range of foodstuffs and other products.[5] If such areas were to be developed with both economic and ecological considerations taken into account they could well contribute substantially to economic growth. And yet, at every point in this process, it is difficult to see anything but benefit to the environment.

Growing forests (unlike mature forests which are in carbon balance) remove carbon dioxide and other greenhouse gasses from the air, and if the timber is used for buildings or furniture then the carbon is effectively "locked-up" for substantial periods of time, and even wood used in fires does not contribute to increases in the overall levels of carbon dioxide in the atmosphere in the way that the use of fossil fuels does. At the same time, even a forest which is being continuously harvested (albeit, at relatively low levels) can provide a substantial habitat for birds and other wildlife; aid in the recycling of nutrients which have been leached deeply into the soil; help to improve water quality and prevent erosion by slowing the rate of run-off after rain; lower water-tables to lessen the problems of salination; and generally aid the long-term fertility (and, therefore, productivity) of agricultural areas further downstream. While the planting, harvesting and transport of the forest products might make some minor contributions to pollution or resource depletion, we could expect these to be completely overshadowed by the contributions to environmental improvement provided by the creation of such areas.

It is not difficult to find other examples where improving overall environmental quality could also make substantial contributions to economic growth and the quality of life—particularly in the long-term. The development of solar and other alternate energy systems, of efficient public transport, of waste recycling industries, of environmentally benign methods of pest control, and of a whole range of anti-pollution devices, to give just a few examples, are all areas where economic development can go hand in hand with ecological concern. Certainly it would be ecologically, as well as economically irrational if policies aimed at restricting economic growth in general were also to restrict growth in areas such as these.

Furthermore, the uncritical critique of economic growth takes little account of the vast difference between the environmental impact of different kinds of industries and industrial practices. It is possible to "develop" an area of rain-forest, for instance, by clearing the valuable timber, burning the rest, and creating (usually fairly unproductive) pasture for beef cattle; or by allowing the development of a much smaller timber industry based on sustainable harvesting, combined with a greater investment in the collection of natural products for pharmaceutical and other uses, and the development of some kind of tourist facilities if appropriate. While it is clear that both such approaches would contribute to economic growth, and both would have an environmental impact, the extent of that impact will be very different, and have vastly different ecological and economic consequences in the long-term. Yet, in the measurement of GDP, no distinction would be made between them.

Much the same can be said of a whole range of other economic activities. Economic growth can be achieved by developing steel production, or petrochemicals, or irrigation schemes, or clothing factories, or service industries, and so on, but the measurement of the general impact of these, in economic terms, takes little or no account of the relative environmental impact of such industries, or even the fact that each of them can be developed in ways which have a greater or lesser effect on local ecosystems. What is vital from an ecological perspective is not the impact of growth as such, but the environmental effects of particular kinds of growth in particular situations. In much of the "developed" world, for example, it is the expansion of the service and information sectors of the economy which have been of most significance for economic growth over recent decades, and while this kind of growth may have some negative effects on the environment, the extent of this effect does not compare with the problems associated with the development of more basic industries: in environmental (as well as other areas) there is a big difference between building a university and a pulp mill.

The point is that if GDP is a poor measure of the real human benefits gained from economic growth, it is even a worse measure of environmental impact. In a sense, to focus on it, or even on economic growth understood in some wider way, is simply to miss the point. The problem is not with economic growth—with expanding our capacity to produce goods—but with determining what goods we really want, and deciding what they are really worth. What this discussion shows is that we have not been very effective at answering either of these questions, and that the economic measures we have used have largely been inadequate for the task they have assumed. What is of real ecological concern is not "growth" or "GDP" but the depletion of non-renewable resources, the pollution of air and water, and the production of waste, and these vary so widely from industry to industry, or economic activity to economic activity, that no general judgements can be made. To focus on an abstractly specified notion of "growth" is to use the kind of intellectual shorthand which not only obscures the real issues, but positively hinders attempts to arrive at solutions. It is, in fact, quite possible to have negative economic growth and a greater impact on the environment, or positive economic growth which is either neutral or actually helps reverse environmental degradation. It is for these reasons that any general attack on growth in-itself does not provide any long-term (or even short-term) solution to the kinds of problems which have arisen from human activities in the world.

Furthermore, one of the major problems of attempting to come to terms with proposals for zero or negative economic growth, even initially, is that it is very unclear what such a program would actually entail. Indeed, short of the most draconian and authoritarian (and unlikely) measures, or a nuclear conflagration, it is difficult to imagine how such a result could be achieved in a world even vaguely resembling our own. And, even if we might wave some magic wand to convert the existing system into one where economic activity was maintained at a constant level, or slowly reduced, it would not really provide an answer to the ecological problems which beset us. After all, in such a world we would still be polluting at a prodigious rate, still eating rapidly into the stocks of non-renewable resources, and still producing mountains of waste. If we accept that our current system of production is not ecologically viable, at least in the long term, and if "zero growth" simply means that we reproduce what already exists, then little or nothing will have been achieved.

While the transition to an ecologically sound economy requires a large scale transformation of our economic system, it is difficult to envisage how such a transformation might occur in a situation of zero or negative growth. At the very least such a transition will require very large scale investment in a range of different areas, and this will not only require growth as a source of the necessary funds, but would also produce growth. Take, for example, the case of energy systems. Currently the great majority of the world's energy is derived from non-renewable and inherently polluting sources: coal, oil or gas are either used directly or burned to produce electricity. While there are cleaner and better ways of doing this than are commonly practiced, even the most effective ways of producing energy using such methods create carbon dioxide—the major "greenhouse" gas—and further deplete the stocks of these non-renewable fossil fuels. Obviously, in the long-term, such methods will have to be replaced by other, more ecologically sound, approaches to energy use. Much, of course, can be done in the way of conservation of energy, but even a very great effort in this area (which itself would require considerable investment) will only reduce—not eliminate—pollution and resource depletion. Nor can we simply turn off the power plants. In our current system of production and distribution this would condemn hundreds of millions of people to misery and death. What we ultimately require is a whole new system of energy use.

While there is every reason to believe that such a system is technologically feasible,[6] even without recourse to nuclear energy, it would require massive changes in both the means of the production of useable energy and the ways in which it is distributed—essentially from a system based on the centralised, large-scale production of energy from the burning of fossil fuels to a decentralised system primarily using solar, wind, water, and biotic sources. And such a transformation can only occur if governments, companies and individuals are willing, and able, to commit the necessary funds over a long period of time. Not only is it highly unlikely that such funds would be committed in a no-growth economy, even if they were, the production of the necessary devices, along with their installation, maintenance and control would all be economic activities contributing to the levels of economic growth. To invest in such a system and maintain zero economic growth requires a double sacrifice: not only would funds be drawn away from alternate avenues for investment, but production in other areas will have to be positively diminished in order to balance the increased production in alternative energy sources. Given that to create an ecologically balanced economy similar changes will have to occur in virtually all other areas of economic life—from agriculture through to information processing—the difficulties of moving towards an ecologically sound society in a no-growth economy seem so great as to be overwhelming. Even if such changes were technologically and economically possible, they require such great sacrifices on the behalf of the population that the chances of the political success of such a program are infinitesimal.

It is true that some might look to a future world, where the transition to an ecologically sound economy has been completed, and suggest that a policy of zero economic growth might be appropriate to such a situation, but this is unlikely to come about either rapidly or easily. Indeed, we have barely begun to move in this direction, and there are many countervailing forces at work. But it is clear that if such a transition is to take place, and if it is to be effective, then it will not involve any diminution or mere maintenance of economic production, but a great surge of activity in a wide range of economic areas. There is, in fact, so much to be done that to talk of a balanced economy, at this stage, is not only inappropriate but counter-productive, not just because it diverts attention away from the vital issues at hand, but because it reinforces the kind of image of green politics as essentially negative which can be used so effectively by its detractors. It is no coincidence that the opponents of the green cause focus so frequently on the supposedly negative economic consequences of environmental policies—it is their best weapon. They can paint images of depression, unemployment and general hardship, because this is precisely what zero or negative economic growth would mean *in our kind of society.*

If the green cause is to gain widespread support then it is unlikely to do so on such a basis. Already, the most vociferous opposition to green policies comes from those whose livelihood is directly affected—whether they be agriculturalists, timber workers, fishermen, miners, industrialists, or those with interests in such activities—and it is unlikely that even the most persuasive ecological rhetoric can readily persuade those who see their incomes and employment disappear because of environmentally based political decisions. We could only expect that such opposition would increase, and increase dramatically, as policies aimed at achieving zero economic growth came to affect much wider sections of the community. But such an approach is as unnecessary as it is impractical. In the immediate, and immediately foreseeable, future the political program of the green movement should not be aimed at the creation of stability (for this would solve nothing in the long-run), but at the transformation of the existing economic order. And rather than this period of transition being a time of depressed economic activity with all that implies—it could well be a period of great activity with significant expansion in particular industries, avenues for investment and employment. More, rather than fewer "goods and services" will need to be produced, even if the nature of these "goods and services" might change significantly. That such a transition will involve sacrifices is clear, but along with these sacrifices come many opportunities, and it is this side of the ecological program which needs to be stressed if its many critics are to be overcome.

Finally, we should not ignore the real benefits which economic growth has, and can continue to provide. To the extent that a developed economic system allows us to meet our needs at a minimal expenditure of time and energy, it opens up the potential to satisfy other needs and wants. It is because we do not have to devote every day to the immediate problems of survival, and because our economic system has provided us with access to vast resources (in comparison to virtually any other period in history), that it is possible for us to devote ourselves to a variety of other tasks and interests. It is easy enough to criticise our "materialist" and "consumerist" society, and to point to the triviality, wastefulness or downright destructiveness of many of the products of the economic system, but that critique should not go so far as to forget that it is the same economic system which also provides us with the potential to provide everyone with comfortable clothing and housing, with adequate food, and with the opportunities to pursue artistic or sporting activities, to travel, to study, to communicate and consult with many others, and even to relax. Wealth (and this is what economic growth provides) is power, and power can be used in creative or destructive ways, and this is true even in regard to the environment.

It is, in a sense, because we are so wealthy that we have the option of ecological concern: that we can devote time and resources to finding and instituting the means of meeting our needs with less environmental impact; that we can act to repair some of the degradations of the past, and that we can afford to forgo opportunities to exploit biotic and mineral resources. Furthermore, it is no accident that the green movement has had its greatest success in richer nations. It is because those nations are wealthy that individuals and groups have access to the scientific and technological resources which have allowed them to uncover many environmental problems, to educate students in the nature of these problems, to communicate their fears to the population at large, to organise into national and international groupings, and to travel and act at more than a local level. The majority of the population of poorer parts of the world do not have such luxuries, and their charges of hypocrisy against the wealthy have all the more force because of this. If the only message we can give them is that they must forego the benefits we enjoy then it should not be unexpected if they treat our communications with disdain. But this is not the only message that can be sent. While we accept that it would be ecologically unsound—if not impossible—for all societies in the world to try to emulate the kind of industrial system characteristic of, say, the USA in 1999, this does not mean that poor societies cannot aspire to a much higher material quality of life. Indeed, the experience of the "developed" nations in environmental areas provides an object lesson in how *not* to develop. But this is the course which will be taken if some other, and better, way is not discovered. These must be the central tasks of the green movement: to bend the direction of economic change in the wealthier nations in a way which takes ecological considerations into account; to show how it is possible to reconcile material well-being with environmental responsibility; and to prove the proposition that an economically rational world is also an ecologically rational world.

This is no small task, and one which will require effective use of the kinds of economic resources which are only available to wealthier nations (which does not, of course, mean that they do not have much to learn from "undeveloped" societies), and any attack on economic growth, in-itself, can only undermine such a process. Nor will it be a short-term task, or one where the ultimate end can be easily envisaged. Any attempt to transform the massive machinery of modern industrial states into something resembling an ecological benign way of meeting our needs not only involves a continuing and drawn-out political and social struggle, but a huge effort in research and innovation. Almost certainly we will learn much in the process, particularly about the multifarious connections between particular kinds of economic activity, human satisfaction and ecological degradation. What will emerge, even if the struggle is successful, is, at best, unclear (and even those who have tried to imagine it have come up with rather different visions), but it is only when great gains have been made in the direction of an environmentally viable society that the question of economic growth even becomes relevant. Hopefully by such a stage we will be in a much better position to provide an answer.

Against the background of the arguments put forward by most environmentalists this analysis might seem both overly optimistic and overly pessimistic: optimistic in its assessment of the possibilities for continued economic development, and pessimistic in its view of the difficulties involved in the transition to an ecologically sound society. But once we abstain from utopian inflected analyses and so abandon the twin assumptions that the present world is in all its forms catastrophically unsustainable, and that our only hope lies in a new "Great Leap Forward", our optimism and pessimism appears as a sensible realism. We do not seek either to gloss-over or ignore problems of transition, nor to underestimate our present resources for managing change.

Notes

1   Jonathon Porritt, *Seeing Green: the Politics of Ecology Explained*, (London: Basil Blackwell, 1990), p. 36.
2   Stephen Jay Gould, *Lifes Grandeur: the spread of excellence from Plato to Darwin*, (London: J. Cape, 1996), pp. 50-55.
3   Cf., Lester Thurow, *The Future of Capitalism*, (Melbourne: Allen & Unwin, 1996), p. 21.
4   Hugh Stretton, "Privatizing and Deregulating", in his *Political Essays*, (Melbourne: Georgian House, 1987), pp. 30-31.
5   Cf., Bill Mollison, with Remy Mia Slay, *Introduction to Permaculture*, (New South Wales: Tyalgum Press, 1991).
6   Amery Lovins, *Soft Energy Paths: Towards a Durable Peace*, (Harmondsworth: Penguin, 1977).

4 Economy and Ecology

The debate about economic growth, which many take to be constitutive of environmentalism, is misguided on both sides. Economic growth *per se* is not the defining point of contrast between ecology and economics. But this is not yet to say that ecology and economics do not stand in fundamental conflict, registering incommensurable ways of viewing human activity in the world. Certainly in most western Governments, for example, there has been, and continues to be, a considerable degree of acrimony between departments responsible for the environment and those concerned with economic management. And in public debates on such issues it is not uncommon to see an ecologist ranged against an economist. In the face of such debates one could easily gain the impression that these two areas of study, or ways of looking at the world, are fundamentally antagonistic. Certainly their proponents often are.

Yet, from a broader perspective, the antagonism is misconceived. Economics and Ecology, after all, are deeply connected, both theoretically and historically, and they have many common roots and shared assumptions. At its most obvious level the extent of this connection can be seen in the words themselves. Both are derived from the Greek *oikos*—meaning "house"—and a literal translation of each—Ecology as "the science of the household", and Economy as "the management of the household"—shows such similarity that we would expect them to be complementary fields. Indeed, the extent of this similarity is so great that *The Shorter Oxford English Dictionary* actually defines Ecology as "the science of the economy of animals and plants". Furthermore, this similarity is not a mere linguistic accident, but an appropriate indication of a real and significant historical connection.

While the logic of their respective meanings might give Ecology some apparent priority, in fact, of the two terms "economy" is considerably older. The study of Political Economy (what we now call Economics) was well established for over a century before the word "ecology" was even coined and, almost certainly, the word was framed with "economics" in mind. Neither study, after all, is really about households as they are commonly understood. With economics this original meaning had gradually come to cover national and even international "households", and it was not an unreasonable extension of meaning to apply it, in Ecology, to the "household" of living things. Moreover, the beginnings of Ecology can be traced directly to Darwin's Theory of Evolution through its originator the German Darwinist Haeckel, and this theory has equally clear connections with the Political Economy of the time. Darwin himself refers explicitly to the classical economist Thomas Robert Malthus as a source of inspiration, and there are obvious similarities between his account of natural selection and Malthus' explanation of scarcity in society. Karl Marx is even reputed to have suggested that "Darwin's theory is merely the application of British Political Economy to the natural world". There is also little doubt that later economists were significantly influenced by their understandings of Darwin.

Among the more influential modern economists, for example, Friedrich Hayek's central notion of the *catallactic* order of the market has much in common with Darwin's views. Both are concerned with the question of how a spontaneous order can arise in the world without the intervention of some external directing force. In economics it is often suggested that this order exists in markets, while in ecology a similar order is displayed in ecosystems. Furthermore, Hayek is very aware of this theoretical connection between the realms of economic and biological theory. He regards his view of *catallaxy,* as well as Darwin's notion of natural selection, as extensions of the idea of spontaneous order which he traces to the social and economic philosopher Bernard Mandeville, and particularly to his *Fable of the Bees*. It is not surprising, therefore, to discover many similarities between economic and ecological thought. Both, for instance, are vitally concerned with the distribution and use of resources, with the conditions which produce stability or equilibrium, and with the role of competition and co-operation in the production of order. Equally, the explanations each offers of these things have much in common. Yet, as we pointed out, in the realm of public policy and political action, those who would see themselves as the followers of these two fields often find themselves at loggerheads. This presents us with a puzzle which deserves further investigation.

At its most fundamental level the disparity between ecology and economics arises from the rather different "households" they are concerned with and this, in turn, leads them to ask rather different questions and to use rather different conceptual apparatus. The "household" that ecology studies is the household of plants and animals and the physical world that surrounds them, and the central questions asked about this household are concerned with the inter-relationships between these organisms and their environment: how can the complex system of life in the world survive? In terms of the Darwinian notions of "natural selection" or the "survival of the fittest", ecologists are less concerned with the history of evolutionary change and more with the characteristics of the "nature" that selects, or the question of what is it that makes particular organisms "fit" into nature. Typically, and particularly in the sub-discipline of "population dynamics", this has led them to focus on the stability of eco-systems. What Malthus had pointed out, and what Darwin had taken up, was the great disparity between the potential and the actual rate of population growth in any species. Given their potential for reproduction, even slowly gestating species like elephants could double their numbers in relatively short periods of time, and then double them again, and so on. But the world is not full of elephants, or mice, or cockroaches. Obviously there must be some mechanism, or set of mechanisms, which prevent such unrestrained growth, and which keeps these species in some sort of balance. Such mechanisms constitute the *balance of nature*.

Given this foundational image it is not surprising to find that the language of ecology is littered with concepts which, in one way or another, are related to notions of stability. The ideas of ecology, particularly in its popularised form, are phrased in terms like "balance", "harmony", "sustainability", or "equilibrium", and even more technical concepts—like the ideas of an "ecological niche" or a "climax state"—carry similar connotations. This encourages an image or vision of the world where stability or balance is the normal or natural state of affairs. Particular ecosystems, in this framework, are judged in terms of how closely they meet this ideal of a stable state. This is, as much as anything, an analytical technique—the base-line of a stable balance is used as a means of understanding actual ecosystems—but it is not uncommon, again particularly in the popular literature, for such an analytic framework to be misinterpreted as a basis for the judgement of value. For many "ecological" writers change is not merely a methodological challenge, it is equated with destruction or, at the very least, a kind of incompleteness which makes for something less than an ideal situation. It is this way of looking at the world which so often places them at odds with economists, for the world-view of economics is a view where change is the norm, and for economists too, fact slides easily into value.

The "household" that is the subject matter of economics is the human household, and while there may be some similarities between this and the study of the "natural" household, there are also some major differences. Almost since its inception, the study of economics has not focused on questions of stability and balance (or at least not in the sense these are understood in ecology), but on questions of change, growth and development. The classical economist Adam Smith, for example, in his *The Wealth of Nations* was concerned to discover how and why societies are able to increase their levels of overall wealth, and this concern as captured by GDP calculations has remained central to the study. Even Malthus, the "dismal parson" revered by some elements of the green movement, did not present an image of the world in terms of stability but only argued that "misery and vice" were inevitable because the growth in the human population (unless it was restrained in vicious or miserable ways) would always outstrip the possibilities for economic (and particularly agricultural) development. Indeed, in his later works his pessimism about the human condition is modified to the extent that he also presents an image of the world in terms of growth and development.[1] Such a dynamic image only becomes problematical when it ignores the background of sustaining conditions necessary for such processes, and while Malthus was never tempted to this mistake, the same, unfortunately, is not true of much of economics which, for a variety of reasons, has tended to emphasise the foreground activities of "Rational Economic Man" at the expense of the broader institutional and natural framework within which activities take place. And it is here the slide from fact to value occurs, for often only change comes to matter, the sustaining conditions of continuity not at all.

One root for this major difference of emphasis, often amounting to a difference in value between economics and ecology is clear enough: it is suggested by the character of the phenomena they observe. An ecologist who studies a mature forest, for example, will observe something like a stable state, where the populations of various species remain relatively constant over long periods of time, and even the instability that might be observed in an area of re-growth will be understood in terms of its movement towards such a stable state. But the phenomena that economists have studied are very different. We must recognise that the development of economics as an area of study, and eventually as a discipline in its own right, essentially took place in Western European nations in the throes of the industrial revolution. If anything, it was the massive social changes which came with that revolution which gave impetus to the development of this area of study. Economics was about the explanation of change, and what is taken as typical or normal is growth, not stability. In the economic world-view periods of relatively stable levels of production (or what are, interestingly enough, called "depressions") are aberrations, and they are explained in terms of their inadequacies in comparison with periods of growth. Where, for an ecologist periods of rapid change indicate some problem with the system, for economists periods of stability present equal difficulties.

What is particularly ironic about this juxtaposition between world-views is that economists can point to precisely the same intellectual source as ecologists for support. The Theory of Evolution, the Darwinist view of the natural world, in which ecology has its basic foundations, can also be drawn on to present an image of the world in terms of growth and development. This theory, after all, is a theory of change, of the evolution of the highly complex and diverse biological world which now exists from earlier, and often simpler, states. Taken in its broadest sense it is a theory of how complexity could emerge out of simplicity, and the processes involved are often akin to those described by students of human economies. The process of specialisation in plants and animals, where-by they use the resources available to them in more effective ways, for example, has obvious parallels in the increasing specialisation of labour which is characteristic of developing economies. Equally, in both biological evolution and economic growth the role of competition can be identified as a major factor which drives development. Comparisons can also be made between the diversification of species and of enterprises, and even the spread of life into new regions can be seen as analogous to the spread of the influence of particular economic groups throughout the world.

That such divergent, even contradictory, images can be drawn from the same source does not indicate any flaw in that source, only its richness as a source of imagery, analogy and explanation. The theory of evolution is about *both* stability and change, and about the relationship between them. Hutchinson[2] expresses this relationship in terms of "the ecological *theatre*" and "the evolutionary *play*", which gives some indication of the dynamics of change and stability within the Theory of Evolution, and also goes some way to explain the diverse visions which can be based upon it. And visions, we should understand, more than detailed analysis, shape public debate. But what is more important is that we can recognise a fundamental connection between "economic" and "ecological" visions of the world, even though they present us with seemingly contradictory images. Where "ecologists" (usually) have concentrated on the theatre, "economists" (again, usually) have focused on the play. They are both concerned with much the same thing, but where the former concentrates on change and movement through time, the latter considers the relatively static structures which ultimately shape those movements. In the terms used above we can say that the orthodox economist is primarily concerned with *foreground* considerations—with the interaction of individuals, where the overall context is taken as given—while the ecologist is concerned with *background* considerations—with the way in which the context in which action takes place both limits and shapes the nature of those actions. This clarification not only helps us to understand why the proponents of these different views often appear to be talking at cross-purposes, it also holds out the possibility of a final reconciliation. At their most fundamental level these world-views are not incompatible but, and necessarily, complementary. The real novelty of environmentalism lies here. For it enables us to recognise and explore this complementarity in an environment where many have chosen one pole at the expense of the other.

Of its nature, complementarity can be approached from either side, but we think it better here to do so from the side of economics. In what follows we show how economics, even if against its inclinations, leads us from a foreground of the market, which is initially considered as entire unto itself, through a recognition of the realities of "negative externalities", to a rather shame-faced acknowledgment of its necessary social and environmental background conditions.

If there is one notion which is central to orthodox economics it is the idea of the *market*, understood as an arena of free (ie. non-coerced) exchange between fundamentally equal actors. The market is seen as the proper means of determining both the allocation of resources to different productive uses and the distribution of benefits and burdens across populations. It is taken to be the proper means of such distribution not only because of its non-coercive character—although this is highly important—but because it is taken to be the most *efficient* means of making these allocations. In this way of thinking market mechanisms are fundamentally superior to other means of resource distribution, and it would only be in the most extreme circumstances that other methods should be considered. Certainly it would not be unfair to suggest that the common response of most orthodox economists to a whole range of questions would be: *by and large everything is best left to the mechanisms of the "free" market.* To understand why they would arrive at this conclusion it helps to consider the typical image of a market.

In its most basic form we might think of a village system of barter. Imagine a simple society made up of a number of independent farmers and artisans: I grow zucchinis, while you keep chickens; Mary weaves wool; Harry builds boxes; Michaelis herds goats; Sean grows potatoes, and so on. Each of us produces more of these things than we need, but not enough of other things that we would like to have (I have become very sick of eating zucchinis and really fancy some chicken—it would also be handy to have a box to carry my produce in). Obviously, we would all be better off if there were some means of redistributing those goods surplus to the owners requirements throughout the population, and the apparently simplest and fairest means of doing this would be through the development of a market. Every Saturday we bring our surplus goods to the village square and proceed to swap goods. I, for instance, swap some of my zucchinis for one of your chickens and then, discovering that Harry doesn't like zucchinis, exchange more for some of Mary's cloth, which Harry will accept for one of his boxes. Such exchanges continue throughout the day, until there are no more exchanges people are willing to make, and then we all go home.

Notice that there is no need for some central authority to distribute goods between us—we make these exchanges freely and in an unpatterned way. Yet the overall result is, in a sense, more *ordered* in that there is now a better match between our wants and the goods we possess than before. This is what Hayek calls the *catallactic* effect of the market: it is a mechanism which spontaneously creates order out of chaos. More, it could be said that the efficiency of the distribution of goods has been improved in every exchange, particularly when we take "efficiency" to have been increased *when one or both parties to an economic exchange perceive themselves to be better off, and neither is worse off.* This is usually referred to as a "Pareto improvement", and the general process one of increasing "Pareto efficiency". Finally, at the end of the day, if we have all bargained assiduously, it could be argued that we have achieved the most efficient possible distribution of goods, reaching a "Pareto optimal" situation—one where *any further exchange would result in someone perceiving themselves as being worse off.* The market, then, has provided a means to maximise efficiency in the *distribution* of goods in a society.

Furthermore, over a period of time, such a market situation also tends to maximise efficiencies of *production.* Here the key mechanism is *competition.* If, for example, it turns out that too many people are growing zucchinis, producing a glut on the market, so their exchange value is decreased, then it only makes sense for me turn to some other kind of product (tomatoes, perhaps) for which there is a high demand. This, assuming I have made the right choice, not only maximises my return for my labour, but also leads to higher levels of production of things that people actually want (otherwise they would not be willing to exchange their goods for them). At the same time, if someone else is a much better zucchini grower than I am, or their land is more suited to the production of zucchinis, then they will be able to undersell me in the market, decreasing my returns. In such a situation it is only rational for me to seek other uses for my talents and lands for which I and they are better suited, or to improve my techniques of zucchini growing in order to compete. Again, market forces produce optimal results. There is a tendency towards the production of goods that people actually want, at the lowest possible price, and towards the use of productive resources (both human and non-human) in their most effective ways.

All of these results have been achieved without any person or group overseeing the process (except, perhaps to maintain the market itself, but we will return to this later), and without any grand design or external authority being imposed on the people. In every case the individuals involved have made their own choices and satisfied their own preferences, as they see them. Maximum social benefit (in the sense of the maximum possible satisfaction of preferences) has been achieved through the pursuit of individual interest. This alchemical process in which the pursuit of private benefits produces benefits for all is what Adam Smith referred to when he spoke of the markets control by a beneficent *invisible hand.*

This is only the image of a market in a very simple form. Real markets, and particularly modern markets, are enormously more complex than this. Even to introduce something as basic as *money* to such a situation radically alters the character and possibilities of the market (it allows, for instance, the *accumulation* of value in ways which are either extremely difficult or impossible in simpler situations). When we consider the proliferation of products in the modern world, the development of national and international trade and monetary systems, and the sheer complexity of economic arrangements in our society, it is clear that we have moved far from such simple market arrangements. Nevertheless, this underlying image of the market, and the fundamental idea of the ultimate efficiency of free exchange have retained their place as the centre-piece of orthodox economics. Indeed, it would be reasonable to suggest that, particularly over the last two decades, it has gained in popularity and influence.

It is also important to recognise the manifest connection between orthodox economics and a dominant—if misguided—*Libertarian* strand of political liberalism. It is no accident that these have common origins and history, nor that the proponents of one were, more often than not, supporters of the other. Both, after all, can be seen as complementary elements of the world-view of the rising, and now dominant, middle-classes. Initially this involved an attack on the arbitrary authority of hereditary monarchies and aristocracies and, more recently, a defence against the claims of socialism and communism. In both the political and economic spheres "individual freedom" became, and remains, the central catch-cry, and for both the central focus of analysis upon which their respective theories have been constructed is that individual. There have also been various attempts to draw definite causal links between "free market" economics and political liberalism, in that freedom in economic life is often seen as a necessary prerequisite for the existence of non-authoritarian political systems.[3] Certainly it is not uncommon for orthodox economists to call on "freedom" (or, more typically, *freedom of choice*) as much as "efficiency" in support of their recommendations. This is an important claim, and one which any attempt to develop a non-authoritarian environmental politics must take seriously. To do this we need to look more closely at some of the assumptions and conclusions of orthodox economics.

According to the orthodox economic world-view, the key economic value is "efficiency", and this value is fundamental to enlightened social thought. We move—ideally—from an inefficient situation to a more efficient one: towards a Pareto optimal situation. The underlying justification of focusing on efficiency in this sense, and elevating it to primacy in social reflection, is that everyone values getting what they want, and nobody wants to be worse off. Economics then, is conceived as an evaluatively neutral calculus for the satisfaction of human wants. But behind this seemingly obvious specification there are (at least) three assumptions which deserve immediate attention:

1. Only human preferences count;

2. There exists a differentiated framework of legally protected property rights (humans can be owners, but not owned; any non-human can be owned);

3. These rights foster certain sorts of exchanges—eg. voluntary, non-fraudulent ones between competent persons.

To uncover these assumptions is to see at once the falsehood of the common claim that economics—at least when it forms the basis for *any* kind of policy proposal—is an entirely value-free or neutral endeavour. Simply to make the most obvious points: it presupposes potentially contentious views about what we value (having our preferences satisfied); about whose preferences count (human beings—in particular, those with something to exchange in the market); and about the background necessary to facilitate this (roughly, a private property and free market community).

Do these evaluative claims withstand scrutiny? Enough has been said about anthropocentrism for you to decide the first point yourselves. Let us turn then to the remaining issues. To begin, consider the notion of efficiency in use, called "Pareto Efficiency", for it is this notion which underlies any claims for the moral acceptability of market relations. As we have seen, a Pareto improvement in a situation occurs when, with none being worse off, some(one) can improve their position, and a Pareto optimal situation is one in which any further exchange would result in someone being worse off.

This may look uncontroversial, but it is more loaded than it appears. We can have serious doubts even about Pareto-optimal situations. For example, a master/slave nexus may be such that it cannot be altered without someone (the master) being worse off. The problem is that the criterion focuses entirely on a given situation and not how it came about. As a consequence there is no room in this style of thought for registering that the master/slave nexus is morally indefensible. In judging the acceptability or desirability of a particular situation we are certainly going to have take into account more considerations than Pareto optimality.

Next, notice that *access to a market presupposes the possession of something which others are willing to pay for.* Many, many millions—human as well as non-human—are in no such position. Arguing that economic efficiency is *the* key notion for enlightened social reflection simply excludes those people (and non-persons) from consideration. And there is a deeper and perhaps even more important worry about whether a free-market, private property economy is the most suited to deliver Pareto improvements. For not only does it effectively exclude many parties from the market, it may happen that even those included in it are typically made worse off through exchanges to which they are not a party. They bear the weight of what are called "negative externalities" or "external diseconomies". This is a particularly significant concern when environmental issues are at stake because, traditionally, the kinds of problems associated with environmental degradation have been seen as "externalities" in just this sense. The overall situation this can lead to is often referred to as "the tragedy of the commons".

In his seminal paper "The Tragedy of the Commons" Garrett Hardin outlines a general situation which can be applied to virtually any of the environmental problems identified in this and other works. It is both an attempt to explain how environmental degradation comes about, and an attempt to put forward realistic suggestions, about how these kinds of problems might be dealt with. The example he focuses upon to make his point is the village "commons", and his argument is concerned with the various pressures placed upon such an area of land, and the results of these pressures.

In the kind of simple village economy we have already described it was very often the case that, apart from land owned or controlled by particular individuals (as in our previous example) there was also a significant area of land set aside for communal use: the village commons. Hardin essentially asks—though he does not put it this way—what happens to such an area if we apply the orthodox logic of the "free market" to its usage? His answer is that an environmental tragedy occurs: the commons is overused, its fertility is not maintained, and eventually it becomes so degraded as to lose its productive capacity. In this case the pursuit of individual self-interest does not maximise efficiency, but ultimately destroys any possibility for the effective use of the available resources. The argument is easy to follow.

If there is such an area of land, available for all to use freely, then it is in the interest of every individual (each rational economic agent) to use it as fully as possible, and to spend as little effort as possible in maintaining its fertility. For every individual farmer it always makes sense, if there is any feed on the commons at all, to run their herds there rather than on their own land, and there are a number of reasons for this. First, by using the commons as well as their own land the farmers, individually, can increase the size of their own herds, and thereby their returns. They have, in effect, a larger area than that which they actually own which they can use. Second, by running their herds on the commons rather than their own lands they reduce the pressure on their own farms, making it easier to maintain fertility and carrying capacity. Third, there is always pressure to use the common resource because, as they do not have exclusive use of it, if they do not reap any potential benefits available from it then somebody else will—they will have lost a possible benefit and may perhaps be subject to feelings of resentment or envy. Finally, and again because they do not have exclusive use, there is no pressure to maintain the fertility in such an area, because the benefits which might result from any particular individual's efforts in this direction could accrue to someone else who also has access to it and has not made such efforts. The result is clear: over time the land will be degraded, and the community as a whole will lose.

The economic forces in operation here can be summed up in simpler and more general terms: *it is always rational for economic actors to privatise benefits and to socialise costs*. That is, in any situation where private benefits (profits) can be gained by particular individuals, but where the costs associated with the production of those benefits can be spread across a broader community, it is always economically "rational" for those individuals to reap such benefits. Even more worrying, this remains the case even when the total benefits produced are considerably *less* than the costs associated with their production (indeed, this remains the case until the point is reached where the costs associated with the activity are so great that the cost to *every* member of the community is greater than the gain to the few individuals involved).

A good example of this process can be seen in the case of something like air pollution, where the air is treated as a commons. Imagine you own a factory which produces widgets (a commodity in high demand in your community), but which also, as a by-product of the cheapest form of production, releases large amounts of pollutants into the air of the city where your factory is located. Imagine, even further, that you have a fairly clear idea of the costs associated with this pollution—in things like greater cleaning bills, losses of agricultural production, and particularly increased medical expenditure. At what point does it become rational for you to either close your factory or invest in pollution control equipment? The answer is, "probably never". This is because, even in the unlikely event that your personal costs associated with the air pollution come to be greater than the profits you gain from the enterprise, you are almost certainly in a position to remove yourself from them by, for example, moving to an area relatively unaffected by the pollution. And this is not a fanciful example: the social and economic demography of virtually any industrial city would serve as empirical evidence.

The same kind of example can be provided for virtually any kind of environmental issue, whether it is pollution more generally, the over-exploitation of natural resources (both renewable and non-renewable), the destruction of wilderness, species extinction, and even rapid population growth. In each case individual self-interest is set against the common good, and the tragedy of the commons looms on the horizon.

We should also recognise that the logic of this situation operates in two directions. It is not just that the economic forces at work operate in ways that are destructive of commons, they also tend to hinder any attempts to improve the situation. So, for example, if you live in a city with high levels of air pollution, and you would prefer this not to be the case, what avenues are open to you in the realm of a free-market economy? Again, the answer is "probably none"—at least if people act in an economically "rational" way. The point is that, even if anti-pollution devices are available (say for cars), it is simply not rational for any particular individual to purchase one. The *cost* of such a purchase is borne by the individual, but the *benefits* are spread across the whole community, and this is not a good bargain. In fact, the overall effects of one person fitting such an anti-pollution device will be negligible—so small as to be unmeasurable, but the costs will be significant. In effect, they will have paid a cost and gained no discernible benefit. The "rational economic agent" of orthodox economics does not operate in such ways.

While a free (ie. non-coercive) market may be very effective in satisfying certain kinds of preferences, meeting the demand for particular kinds of goods, the example of the "tragedy of the commons" shows us that there is also a whole class of preferences which it simply cannot satisfy. In particular, the market is a very poor mechanism for providing for those preferences *which can only be satisfied through collective action*. Most environmental preferences fit into this category. Our individual attempts to ameliorate the problems associated with pollution, resource depletion, the destruction of wilderness, and so on, only take on any significance if other people also make such attempts. Our individual preferences (for clean air etc.) in such cases, can only be satisfied by communal action.

The realisation that often we can only achieve what we want through collective action puts paid to the orthodox economics claim to monopolise the concept of freedom, in particular the freedom liberal politics sought to secure. The freedom economists focus on is a freedom in the foreground, thus the emphasis on freedom of choice. But sometimes freedom of choice on this level is a curse not a blessing. To give a simple illustration, consider Greg. Greg likes a drink or two at the hotel, but reliably after six drinks he becomes violent and often runs afoul of the judiciary. For Greg, short-term freedom of choice leads to restricted, often unpleasant, choices in the future. So Greg has an idea. He asks the local publicans to refuse him a sixth drink, knowing that after five drinks he will certainly then want a sixth, and will appeal to his right to freedom of choice when refused. The publicans, being tough but caring fellows, agree. Greg has less freedom of choice immediately—he can't choose now to purchase a sixth drink—but greater freedom overall in that he has available more, and more worthwhile choices than before. He has exercised his freedom to shape the background conditions of foreground choice so as to further his freedom. And he has done so not by personal decision alone, but through the coordinated efforts of others.

This liberating possibility of furthering freedom by organising those background conditions out of which the possibilities of choice emerge and against which they appear is implicitly recognised by virtually all of us in our lack of debate on the compulsory nature (if not the amount) of Government taxation. To argue that freedom would be furthered by making contributions voluntary is to ensure the destruction of that background of agreed coercion against which freedom of choice becomes something more than being forced into desperate alternatives. As Hardin did not have to teach us, a system of voluntary taxation is soon no system at all, just as a system of environmental management which obsessively insists on freedom in the foreground, is no system of management, but a competitive rush to disaster.

The trouble many find in appreciating this dismal logic lies in the general orientation of economics as a field of study. As we pointed out earlier, economics has typically focused on foreground rather than background considerations. That is, it has primarily been concerned with the behaviour of economic actors in certain kinds of institutions, and considerably less with the more general context in which such activity takes place. The consideration of such contexts was generally taken to be the subject of other disciplines. So, for example, it is only very recently that there has been any attempt to take natural resources into consideration when national accounts are calculated. This meant that countries like Costa Rica were seen as having rapidly growing levels of prosperity, even when much of this prosperity was based on the destructive logging of rainforests. The monetary income was measured, but the fact that the resource which generated this income was rapidly declining was not taken into account. The natural environment, if you like, was taken as a given.

If we take the notion of "the tragedy of the commons" seriously, consideration of such "givens" becomes of central concern, and the implications of this for our approach to social and political life, as well as economic activity itself, are wide-ranging and significant. These issues are the concern of the following chapters.

Notes

1   For a more detailed account of these points see David Wells, "Resurrecting the Dismal Parson: Malthus, Ecology and Political Thought", *Political Studies*, 1982, XXX:1, pp.1-15.

2   Hutchinson, G.E., *The Ecological Theatre and the Evolutionary Play*, (New Haven: Yale University Press, 1965).

3   Hayek's highly influential *The Road to Serfdom*, for example, is an explicit defence of this position.

5 Commons, Community and Environment

In the previous chapter we pointed out that virtually every environmental problem can be seen as an instance of a "tragedy of the commons", and that understanding environmental issues in this way has a variety of social, economic and political implications. Before examining these in any detail it is necessary to look at the nature of commons, and the "tragedy" associated with them, in considerably greater depth. For, while Hardin may have identified the general characteristics of commons and the processes involved in their degradation, there are a number of areas where his analysis does not go far enough, and this is often in areas where a more detailed consideration of the issues involved would lead to rather different conclusions.

To begin with we need to make a distinction between what might be called "free" commons and "communal" commons. The first of these refers to those commons which, although they are used by people, have been so abundant that there was no reason (or even thought) that access to them, or use of them, should be restricted in any way: they are not considered to be *property*. The second refers to those commons which are also used by people, but where supply is restricted, and a form of communal ownership exists: they are perceived as *community property*. A good example of the first (at least for most people, for most of human history) would be the air. This is vital to our existence, and we all use it, but (at least until recently) it was available in such abundant and pure supplies that is could be freely used, and it would not have made sense to think of it as even communal property. A good example of the second would be something like a public sporting field. While people might have access to the use of such a field, the nature of their use, and the degree of their access is limited in a variety of ways (I cannot, for instance, dig up the football pitch to grow zucchinis). In most cases such facilities would be considered as publicly or communally owned, as opposed to being owned by particular individuals.

This is an important distinction, but we should also recognise that it is not totally clear-cut. Rather, "free" and "communal" commons represent poles on a continuum, and many of the commons we use could best be placed somewhere between these extremes. And the particular position in which they are placed may depend on a variety of factors. A body of water which serves as the harbour for a large metropolitan centre, for example, is likely to be treated more as a communal rather than a free commons, while the opposite will likely hold for an equivalent body of water in a largely uninhabited region. Between these poles there may be a variety of different levels of usage of waterways, requiring different levels of communal control. And the extent to which we might label these as "free" or "communal" commons will vary with these factors.

We should also recognise that the extent to which such commons are treated in these ways has a connection with their degree of visibility, at least from an economic point of view. For while in most economic thinking commons are taken to be a part of the background, and therefore relatively invisible to analysis, some will be more visible than others. Thus the sporting field or harbour we have already mentioned might well register with the orthodox economist (if only in their peripheral vision) as foci of other kinds of economic activity, where the "free" commons of an unused inlet or wilderness area will hardly register at all. Having no direct or obvious impact on the foreground of the market "play" they remain an unnoticed, and unvalued surrounding "theatre".

Nevertheless, and even with these qualifications, the distinction between "free" and "communal" commons remains vital for our consideration of the "tragedy of the commons". This is because there is a delicious irony in Hardin's analysis of the situation.

The core of his argument can be restated as an account of what happens when market forces are involved in the exploitation of a "free" commons. Hardin himself makes neither of these qualifications. His "tragedy of the commons" is presented as the tragedy of *all* commons—a generality which means that any distinction between market and non-market approaches, or between "free" and "communal" commons, is obliterated. Yet, the example he uses, of the village commons, if considered as real historical entities, rather than as abstract models of economic analysis, provides us with one of the best possible illustrations of environmental preservation rather than degradation. The point is that such commons actually existed and *they were not destroyed.* Indeed, they persisted for centuries as fertile and productive areas, and the eventual destruction of most of them did not come about through the processes Hardin describes, but by the combination of quite different political and economic forces. Hardin's paradigm for understanding environmental breakdown turns out, in fact, to provide a model for environmental management.

This ironic twist arises primarily because Hardin does not make the distinction between "free" and "communal" commons. In fact, it is only in one of the proposed solutions to the "tragedy" he envisages, and then only implicitly, that he recognises the existence of "communal" commons at all. In this he is not alone. Rather, and although his professional training was as a biologist, in this he simply reflects the predominantly individualist and economistic orientation of his own, and much of western society. In such a world-view, as we have already pointed out, the notion of the communal provision of communal goods cannot readily take root. Faced with the existence of commons, they can only be identified as "free" commons, because the rational, self-interested individual of much of economic theory and liberal political philosophy is not a communal creature, but a seperate entity for whom property rights attach, and can attach, only as a private possession. Hardin provides us with a very clear account of the destructive pressures on "free" commons as a means to draw our attention to a whole range of environmental issues, and in this his analysis is correct, precisely because most environmental resources have essentially been treated as "free commons" subjected to the unrestrained exploitation of the market. But his prime example—the basis on which he builds his argument—does not fit into this category.

Equally, and because of this general orientation, Hardin never asks a more fundamental question: *why were there village commons in the first place?* After all, from his own analysis, the existence of such areas is clearly environmentally, socially and economically dysfunctional: they are doomed to destruction by the inexorable logic of overuse. If this were the case then it becomes very difficult to understand how they could have arisen or, if they did, how they could have persisted for long enough to provide most of us with even the concept of their existence. If village commons were the failed experiments which Hardin's arguments suggest they should have been, then it is unlikely that any but a few medieval historians would have heard of them. Yet they are not an unfamiliar concept, even for those of us who do not live in countries where areas of common land are identified in this way.[1] This suggests to us that "commons" are of considerable cultural significance, and to understand why this is we shall consider their nature and historical context in more detail.

The village commons Hardin impugns were primarily a medieval institution, typically, although not exclusively, associated with the small-scale agricultural life-style of peasant communities. In such situations the pattern of land-use was basically determined by custom and tradition. However, the pattern of this usage was far more complex than that imagined by Hardin. Rather than individuals having their own holdings—the kind of system of distinct and individually owned "farms" that we would find familiar—the more typical arrangement was what is usually referred to as the "common field" system. That is, apart from the village "commons" itself, the land was divided into a number of large fields. These, in turn, were divided into numerous smaller plots or "rows". Each farming family was entitled to the use of a number of these rows, spread out among the various fields. Each of these *fields* was then rotated in its use—typically fallow, roots, legumes, and then grains.

At the same time there were (often quite extensive) areas of land set aside for common use—the village commons—and certain kinds of rights also existed to the use of much larger areas. Apart from the commons, for example, local forests were often used as sources of food and fuel (although the way these were used was strictly regulated: peasants might take their pigs into the forest to feed on acorns at particular times of the year, but it would have been a crime for them to kill a deer or chop down a tree—an early form of environmental regulation). There existed a system of different kinds of rights to different kinds of land usage, ranging from the exclusive use of particular plots (although the decision as to what would be grown in them in any particular year was decided communally), to limited (but general) rights to the use of the village commons, and even more strictly limited rights to the use of other areas.

It is important to recognise that these were rights of *usage*, based on custom and tradition, not of *ownership* in the kind of formal or legal sense we understand it today. For while these rights had been entrenched over centuries, and had the force of law within these communities, they were not taken to be (as was subsequently, and often tragically, to be shown) the kind of rights which we now associate with the ownership of property. It is also important to recognise that these rights, and the duties, obligations and institutions connected with them, were not the product of some centralised or planned social vision, but of a slow, and largely internally driven process of social and cultural evolution. This history has been outlined by Chesterton[2] in a way that is particularly pertinent to our discussion, and it is useful to follow his argument at some length.

He points out, as a beginning, that the origin of such medieval communities was usually in the earlier institution of slavery:

> What we call the manors were originally the *villae* of the pagan lords, each with its population of slaves. Under this process ... what had occurred was the diminishment of the lord's claim to the whole profit of a slave estate, by which it became a claim to the profit of part of it, and dwindled at last to certain dues or customary payments to the lord, having paid which the slave could enjoy not only the use of the land, but the profit of it.[3]

This, according to Chesterton, was essentially a process of increasing freedom, where-by the original slave is slowly transformed into a "peasant proprietor". The intermediate stage was one of *serfdom*: where the duties and obligations of the peasant to the lord were matched with particular rights and obligations of the lords to the peasants. Again, these systems of rights and obligations were developed and extended over time until the role of the original slave became something quite different. As Chesterton puts it: "at the end he really had become a small landlord, merely because it was not the lord that owned him but the land".[4]

As Chesterton understood it, this is not just a story of individual emancipation but of communal development. Such communities evolved in the long "Dark Ages" that followed the fall of the Roman Imperium. And the social and cultural evolution which took place was a response to the particular problems which faced such communities. The process was not just, even mainly, a granting of formal freedoms as a product of political pressures, but the gradual growth of a freer society, grounded in the institutions and customs of community life, and it was in these institutions and customs that the rights and duties associated with freedom were embodied. Among the most important of these institutions, and a primary focus of both rights and duties were the "Common Field" system and the institution of the "Common Land".

Yet, from a twentieth century point of view, these are very strange institutions indeed, seemingly both inefficient and clumsy. It is in considering *why* such seemingly strange institutions evolved that we begin to glimpse the answer to those questions about the role and significance of commons which Hardin did not ask, and to find some clues as to why the "tragedy of the commons" he describes did not take place. For while we may suspect Chesterton of a somewhat romantic view of medieval life in general, and peasant life in particular, he has identified one of the major (although certainly not the only) functions of commons in society. They are, if you like, a form of general social insurance. Again, he is worth quoting at some length:

> Medievalism believed in mending its broken men: and as the idea existed in the communal life for monks, it existed in the communal land for peasants. It was their great green hospital, their free and airy workhouse. A Common was not a naked and negative thing like the scrub or heath we call a Common on the edges of the suburbs. It was a reserve of wealth like a reserve of grain in a barn; it was deliberately kept back as a balance, as we talk of a balance at the bank.[5]

We must remember that the primary activity, the focus of life and the basis for continued existence in such societies was agriculture. And agriculture is an inherently risky activity. The vagaries of seasons and extremes of weather, the periodic destruction caused by blights and diseases, as well as the many disruptions brought on by social and political events, combine to render the products of labour uncertain: in some years abundance; in others a shortfall. Moreover, these boons and banes do not always fall evenly: the freak storm that destroys one peasant's crop may merely water another's. The existence of the commons was a means of managing such risks and of evening out such fluctuations—for both individuals and communities.

In poor seasons, or in cases of individual disaster, the resources of the commons could be drawn upon to sustain life and to provide a basis for regeneration. In periods of abundance these resources could be allowed to accumulate to provide a buffer against future calamities. The commons were a means for the communal provision of communal goods: they provided a kind of security for both individuals and groups which could not be provided in a pure market situation. And the "Common Field" system performed a similar function. Because particular individual's plots were not concentrated but spread widely, and mixed with the plots of others, both disasters and abundances were spread more evenly in the first place. It was unlikely, then, that anyone would be so reduced by fortune as to be forced into penury or so fortunate as to rise far above the others. For the resources of particular individuals were both backed by, and bound up with, the resources of the community as a whole. Furthermore, because the fields were rotated commonly, they could be more effectively used as areas of common grazing after harvest, and such grazing is more efficient on larger areas.

Apart from their vital economic function the commons also served as a focus for community life in general. They were the recreation grounds, the sites for festivals and entertainments, and a place where people could meet and engage in general social intercourse. Equally, because individual plots were in common fields, peasants often worked together or in close proximity, and there was both the opportunity and good reason for co-operation. In a real sense they were the foundation for the communal existence of peasant society. Indeed, it would not be unreasonable to suggest that such communities existed precisely *because* these kinds of commons existed. In the process of development from slave estate to peasant village the creation of commons was not merely a contingent afterthought, it was a necessary condition. And because of this very necessity, the management and preservation of the commons was a central element of local governance.

For such communities were not only largely autonomous as economic units, they were also, to a significant degree, autonomous political units. They were, to be sure, subject to a variety of higher authorities, both secular and religious, but very many of the functions we now associate with the centralised institutions of modern states were performed and controlled at a local level. And among the most important were those concerned with the maintenance of the common resources of the village, and here the common lands were only the most obvious part. Apart from these there were also systems of roads, lanes and bridges which allowed the movement of people, produce and flocks from one area to another, and which were supplemented by a variety of different drainage systems and levee banks to control flooding and drain marshy areas and numerous fences and hedgerows which (given the patterns of land-use) were frequently maintained in common. In the villages themselves there was usually a market square and, very often, some kind of communal hall or meeting place. The village church also had something of this character.

So, even in the very simplest communities there were a variety of commons which were basic not only to the economic but also to the communal life of such societies. And the use, maintenance and improvement of such commons was a central element of communal existence. Such commons were preserved over time through the evolution of quite complicated systems of right, duties and obligations. Some of these were upheld in relatively formal ways (in the processes for solving disputes, for example), but the great majority were enshrined in customs upheld by the forces of social expectation. In such face-to-face societies, to shirk your duty, or to impinge on the rights of another, was to undermine your own standing and reputation and, in extreme cases, might even lead to one's effective banishment as the general support and protection of the community was withdrawn. Equally importantly, this system of rule was not imposed from the top down, but evolved from the bottom up, as both a precondition and a consequence of the evolution of original slave estates into peasant communities.

There is much more which could be said about the nature of such communities (and the wider society in which they were embedded was far more complicated than this), but the general point is that such communities existed for centuries and that, rather than being sites of degradation and destruction, the commons persisted as viably sustainable and focal features of community life. In fact, so central were such commons that the ultimate destruction of many of them was also the destruction of the communities themselves.

The tale of this destruction is too long and tragic to be told here, but it essentially involved the reassertion of aristocratic property rights, the enclosure of the land, and the dispossession of the peasantry.[6] Lands which had been the "property"—in the sense of exclusive rights of usage—of particular families for hundreds of years, as well as the communal "property" which all could use, were transferred by a variety of political (and often violent) means into the formal property of large land-holders, and the peasants reduced to the status of agricultural day-labourers, all too willing to move to the cities and the "dark satanic mills" of the emerging industrial society. The "tragedy of the commons" did not come about through the dynamics of over-use and exploitation within the communities which shared them, but through the forcible destruction of those communities by means of the appropriation of their common holdings.

This is a very different story to the one told by Hardin, and one with rather different implications. It does not, for instance, lead us to the conclusion that a "commons" situation is one to be avoided as a sure route to disaster. Rather, it suggests that what is important is that commons should be recognised as, and treated as, communal resources, in much the same way as commons were treated in the medieval communities we have described—that the "free" commons of the environment which we have drawn on in unthinking, and often destructive ways, need to be perceived as "communal" commons, and managed appropriately. What remains to be considered is whether such an apparently "medieval" institution could find any place in the very different societies in which we now live. To do this we need to look at the significance and treatment of commons in our own societies.

Commons, even understood in Hardin's limited sense, have never fully disappeared. As Elinor Ostrom displays in her *Governing the Commons*,[7] there are many and varied examples of "common resource regimes" throughout the developed and less developed worlds. These range from ground water users associations in California to fisheries in Maine and Turkey; from irrigation systems in Spain and the Philippines to high pasture management in Switzerland and Japan. Some of these have developed in relatively recent times (as in California) but others (as in Spain and Switzerland), and *contra* Hardin, have persisted in largely unchanged forms for many centuries. Indeed, given that some of these systems of communal management are at least 500 years, and possibly as much as 800 years old, they have shown an amazing adaptive resilience, both politically and environmentally, through long periods which were often characterised by social, economic and political turbulence. But even Ostrom's examples are only of the most obvious (and typically agricultural) forms of commons management. The closer we look, even at highly industrialised societies, the more we recognise the sheer pervasiveness of commons in all of our lives.

The first point that needs to be made in any consideration of commons in modern societies concerns their relative *invisibility*. This is particularly obvious in relation to environmental commons. In market-oriented, and essentially liberal, political and social systems, the physical and biological environment which surrounds us and sustains us has rarely been a primary focus for consideration. Indeed, before the rise of modern environmentalism we have to go back to the works of Malthus to find a main-stream theorist who gives the environment (understood in this way) any central role at all. For the great majority of social, economic and political theorists the environment has been taken as a given, and their attention has been directed to other things. It is the partial achievement of the environmental movement that serious economic and political thought must bring the environmental background in to the foreground of reflection. This, of course, is not an easy task. As we pointed out in the previous chapter, the analytic techniques of most mainstream economists and liberal political theorists, with their focus on individual choice and action, are not well suited to the consideration of such "background" issues. However, once we recognise the significance of the background then we begin to see the importance of commons in our own society, and the degree to which they have been overlooked.

Consider the market itself. This is generally taken to be an arena of individual choice in the pursuit of individual preferences: there is no commons *in* the market. Yet, from a deeper, "ecologically informed", perspective, the market *is* a commons. And this is not just in the trivial sense that markets, very often, were held on areas of common land, but in the fundamental sense that a system of market relations *requires* an institutional foundation which is (and *must be*) a commons. In particular, there must be a system of law, and the institutions to uphold that law, in order for any market system to operate—and these can only be understood as kinds of commons.

"Free" choice and "free" exchange depend upon the existence of a set of enforceable rules if they are to be maintained, of which the most important are those rules which protect property, enforce contracts and prevent fraud. Without such rules the market cannot operate. So, for example, it is rather difficult to see how a market could arise in a culture which did not have a strong sense of private property. If there is no clear distinction between what is mine and what is yours then exchange becomes meaningless. In such a situation people do not bargain, they simply share, willingly or otherwise. And much the same point can be made about the need to enforce contracts and prevent fraud. If people do not have to keep their promises then there is little basis for exchange or bargaining. Furthermore, these rules must be more than just cultural predilections, they must be reliably enforceable if people are to have the kind of confidence in fair dealing which encourages them to bring their goods to the market in the first place. If theft, fraud or bad faith cannot be redressed, and redressed in a way which is perceived as fair to the parties involved, the market cannot persist.

If there is to be a market, there must be some kind of legal system and some kind of law enforcement agency. And these are commons: they are maintained by the community, and (at least ideally) are accessible to all. And it is clear that these are not minor or peripheral aspects of modern societies. There are highly developed and continually evolving legal systems and a variety of publicly funded agencies, largely devoted to maintaining the conditions under which free and fair exchange in the market can take place. There is also a more fundamental sense in which this can be understood. In our kind of society we maintain and encourage market systems of exchange precisely because the existence of such markets is taken to be a common good (this, after all, is the basic economic justification for markets). But we also recognise that this "common good" is not one which can, itself, be provided by the market (we would not, for instance, want a privately owned system of law enforcement). Again, this is an area where we must rely on the communal provision of communal goods. The lesson is apparent: *private enterprise rests on communal foundations.*

This general point can be taken even further. It is not just that commons are fundamental to free-market economics, they also form the foundations of political liberalism as well. Much the same point can be made here: the individual freedoms found in liberal societies can only exist because there is the commons of the legal system to protect and maintain those freedoms.[8] And, just as importantly to the existence of liberal society, the system and institutions of government are also a commons. It is not just that the "rule of law" is fundamental to liberalism (although it certainly is), but that the means of determining those laws is also communal. The system of democratic, and particularly parliamentary, government is also, and clearly, a commons: something maintained by the community, accessible to the community, and justified in terms of the common good. Indeed, much of the history of the development of liberal politics can be seen precisely as a history of the wresting of governance from the *private* hands of monarchs and aristocrats into the *public* or *communal* hands of the people—in the name of the "common good". Again the lesson is apparent: *liberal individualism rests on communal foundations.*

So far, then, we have identified some fundamental commons in liberal and basically free-enterprise societies. The first of these are those environmental commons which are basic to the existence of any kind of society at all. The second are those basic institutional commons which lie at the foundations of our particular kind of society. Both of these kinds of commons, therefore, can be seen as *constitutive*. By this we simply mean that they are essential to the existence of society in general, and of our kind of society in particular. But the role of commons in society, and ours in particular, does not end here. Indeed, the more we examine the background of social existence, the more we discover commons.

The most obvious of these are the *tangible* and frequently *economic* commons which abound in developed societies. Consider the transport system in such societies. While there may be some elements of private ownership in such systems (and the extent of this varies greatly between different countries), the viability of these, and of the systems themselves, rests upon the existence of a variety of communal commons. So, for example, a system of public roads—regulated, owned, constructed, maintained and useable by the community—is a vital component of any developed economic system.[9] As in the medieval villages, the existence of a market depends upon the existence of means of transporting goods to and from that market. And the same point can be made about other forms of transport: navigable waterways and air space, to give just two major examples, are generally held and treated as commons. Furthermore, in many societies, other major elements of the transport system are also communally owned, in the form of things like public rail and bus companies, airlines and shipping lines.

In fact, the basic economic infrastructure, of transport, communications and, very frequently, energy systems, along with such vital services as water supply, sewage services and garbage collection, are either communally owned or depend upon the communal ownership and control of other commons in virtually all societies. So, for example, even if a telecommunications system is operated by private organisations, the airwaves themselves are still communally owned, and must be communally controlled if there is not to be chaos. At the very basis of the economic activity of virtually all economic systems, then, there are a host of commons which, in a very real sense, form the foundations for economic life in general. Without the existence of such commons the system could not function.

Apart from such direct economic commons, there are also numerous, if not so direct, commons which are vital not only to the economic system, but to the maintenance of a reasonable social existence. The most obvious of these can be found in the areas of health, education and welfare. While in each of these areas there is a significant private component, it is the commons in each which is of most significance in the provision of the desired goods. Consider, for example, the area of health. Here there is an obvious private component: the private practitioners, hospitals and health insurance funds. But there are also significant, and vital commons. These do not just exist in the many public practitioners, hospitals and insurance schemes but, and most importantly, in the system of public health itself. For it is clear that the great advances in improving the health of particular populations which have taken place in the last century have largely been the product of the provision of public goods. In particular, the provision of clean and potable water and the construction of effective sewage systems in cities and towns, have done more for the health of the general population than the many advances in medical science which have also occurred in this period. And notice that even when those advances in knowledge, such as the development of vaccines for serious diseases like polio, have had spectacular effects, this has primarily been because of their widespread, and publicly funded distribution.

Much the same point can be made in the areas of education and welfare. While there are also significant private components in these areas, the great advances in the general levels of education and economic security (for welfare systems can be seen as a form of public insurance against poverty) came about when there was significant public and community investment in these areas. Further, the public provisions of such goods was designed with both economic and social aims in mind. While there are obvious economic advantages to be gained by raising the levels of health, education and security in society, these are also taken to be general social goods. It is not just that the existence of a healthy, educated and secure work-force benefits the economy, though that is certainly true, it is that these things are taken to be worthwhile in their own right. To improve them is to improve our social existence, even apart from any economic benefits which might also follow.

Nor does the role of commons in society end here. Perhaps the most important commons are those which are the least tangible, and the least visible: what we might call *cultural* commons. A society is much more that its physical and economic infrastructure. These might well form a significant basis for social existence, but they are not sufficient by themselves. What is also, and necessarily, required is a system of common understandings through which we can relate to each other, understand each other, and act in concert. It is, for instance, because we have a common language (or languages) that social life, as we understand it, is possible in the first place. It is also through the use of language that we have created, and can preserve, and continue to build, the most important resource of all—knowledge.

It is clear that the kinds of societies which have developed in the West since the beginnings of the industrial revolution owe much to the associated development of scientific and technological knowledge in a variety of different areas. And we are not just referring here to the "pure" sciences, or the developments in mechanical, electrical and electronic technology (although these are obviously highly important), but also to the much broader general areas of theoretical and practical knowledge which underlie the majority of our social and economic activities. At one end of this broad spectrum we might point to the revolutionary developments in theoretical physics, while at the other we might consider the more mundane activities of accountancy, plumbing or motor mechanics. What is apparent in all these cases, and any intermediate ones as well, is their dependence on the existence of a common store of knowledge which has developed over ages, and to which we are still continuing to contribute.

All societies, from the most apparently "primitive" to the most technologically sophisticated, are built upon such commons of knowledge: they are the basis of our survival. The techniques of hunting and gathering, of agriculture in all its forms, of manufacture—whether of the simplest tools or the most sophisticated computer systems, and even of social organisation itself, are essential cultural artefacts upon which all societies and individuals draw in order to ensure their continued existence. They form a series of overlapping and interconnected commons which are fundamental to our lives. Without these stores of knowledge (resources which are, in a sense, inexhaustible), we would be simply another omnivore (and, most likely, extinct). Yet, these are commons which are, by-and-large, taken for granted in social, political and economic analysis. And, even when they are mentioned (in analyses of the significance of research and development, for example), their character and significance as commons is rarely mentioned.

Yet, these must be understood as commons, even though there may be many examples where access to them has been restricted in some way. The medieval guilds, for example, went to some pains to preserve the secrets of their crafts, and modern corporations are often loathe to share their technical expertise—particularly with competitors. But, even in such cases, the knowledge involved can still be considered in terms of the commons. This is most obvious in the case of the guilds. For they must be understood as communities, and communities *based on* the existence of a commons of knowledge. They could be guilds because they could restrict access to the skills and understandings involved in their enterprise, and one of their major functions as guilds was the preservation and development of such knowledge. Again, we can see an intimate connection between commons and communities. And even in the case of modern corporations anxious to preserve industrial secrets we can see a commons at work. Here the key mechanism is the patent system. While new industrial processes and technologies might be kept secret for limited periods of time, this can never continue for ever, and it soon becomes necessary to protect such knowledge through the application for a patent. But what such an application requires is the disclosure of this knowledge in exchange for rights over the use of the product or process. The knowledge itself becomes part of the public domain, and can be used *as knowledge* by anyone, even while there are restrictions on the use of the particular process or product: the commons of knowledge has been expanded, and this is taken to be a communal good (the basic justification for the system). So, even in cases where there is an apparent restriction on common use, we still find a commons in operation.

Rather than "commons" being outmoded medieval institutions, doomed to destruction by the forces of individual economic "rationality", they are, as systems for the communal maintenance and regulation of common resources, pervasive, and vital, aspects of our own societies. At every level of human life, from the most direct requirements of physical life, to the arenas of economic and political activity, and even of culture itself, we are constantly involved with commons of one kind or other. Their seeming "invisibility" is not a consequence of their rarity, but of their familiarity. They are, in a sense, so familiar and so pervasive, so much a part of the background of our lives, that we tend to ignore them and forget them, in precisely the same way that the environmental commons, which form the background to all life and human activity, have been ignored and forgotten in the rush for economic development. In focusing our attention so exclusively on the foreground of change and development, we have often lost sight of the common, ecological, foundations upon which these are built.

Moreover, when we come to examine commons, we do not find discrete entities, but overlapping and interconnected systems. For, while it is often convenient to categorise commons in particular ways—as "free" or "communal", "tangible" or "intangible", "environmental", "economic", "political", "social" or "cultural" commons—such labels do not refer to distinct and separate "things", but to attributes, and attributes which are never absolute, but always a part of some continuum. Consider, for example, an area of relatively pristine wilderness, preserved as a "national park". This, fairly obviously, could be designated as an "environmental" commons, and treated as such. Yet even such an area, one where human activity and impact is minimal, might well serve a variety of functions, acting as a different kind of commons for different purposes. So, for example, such an area might serve as a watershed: a source of clean water which, further downstream, is then used for a variety of domestic, agricultural and industrial uses. In such cases it would not only have the character of an "environmental" commons, but of an "economic" commons as well. Furthermore, in its recreational uses we might well see the existence of a "social" commons, while in its role as an area of scientific study, and also as a source of aesthetic enjoyment and inspiration, would identify it as a "cultural" commons. And it may have any of these attributes to a greater or lesser extent. An area of great environmental significance, natural beauty and scientific interest, for example, may be so remote (like Antarctica) as to have little direct recreational or economic use. There is, in short, no clear or precise distinction between "environmental" commons and other kinds of "commons", either conceptually or practically.

This point is important for our discussion because it is this recognition, along with our understanding of the relationship between commons and communities, which allows us to forge a clear linkage between what are usually taken to be the specific concerns of "environmentalists" and those issues which have been the major foci of more "traditional" approaches to politics. It has been one of the great weaknesses of much of green social and political theory that the connection drawn between concern with the environment and more traditional political concerns—like "justice", "equality" and "freedom", for example—either fail to stand up to serious examination (as with Hardin from the right, or Bookchin from the left), or are, in a sense, simply arbitrary (as, for instance, with Eckersley). To recognise the general significance of commons, for environmental, as well as economic, political and moral issues, in contrast, provides us with a means to develop an integrated and viable account of a genuinely green politics. A politics which, with its focus on the "theatre" of common life over the details of the foreground "play", deserves to be called *Political Ecology.*

Notes

1   In Australia, for example, the more usual term would be "reserve"—which has a significance in its own right.
2   The relevant sections are to be found in Chesterton's *A Short History of England*, reprinted in Chesterton, G.K., *The Essential G. K. Chesterton*, (Oxford: Oxford University Press, 1987), pp. 361-410.
3   *Ibid.*, p. 390.
4   *Ibid.*
5   *Ibid.*, p. 391.
6   A reassertion which often began with the major local property owners unilaterally enclosing areas of the local commons, then appealing to aristocratic authority to "legitimate" the usurpation.
7   Elinor Ostrom, *Governing the Commons*, (Cambridge: Cambridge University Press, 1998).
8   Another (and particularly significant) way of putting this is to point out that at the foundations of even the most individualistic forms of liberalism there is a commons of *moral consideration* which is the basis of liberal freedom.
9   And even when there are private components in such a system (eg. a privately owned toll bridge), these components can only function because of the existence of a wider, publicly owned, system. There would be no point in having a bridge if there were no roads to service it.

6 Political Ecology and the Social Contract

Political ecology is essentially a politics of the commons, in the same way that traditional Liberalism is frequently characterised as a politics of "freedom", or Socialism as a politics of "equality". The central problem for the political ecologist, if you like, is "how do we solve the tragedy of the commons?"

At first glance this may appear to be a difficult, even impossible task. In the years in which we have taught in this area we have found that it is not uncommon for students, so bemused by the apparently inexorable logic of the "tragedy", to throw up their hands in despair at this point, or to seek solace in what are often highly authoritarian responses. But this indicates more about common cultural attitudes and understandings of the "public" and the "political" than it does about the real difficulty of the task (and that such attitudes are so prevalent is itself an important point). The very fact that we can point to numerous historical and contemporary examples of functional and sustainable "resource management regimes" should be cause for some optimism. However, our task at this point is not to look in detail at the kind of institutional arrangements which Ostrom considers (although we will return to these), but to look further into the "deep logic" of the "tragedy". The most convenient point to begin this investigation is through a consideration of the "solutions" which Hardin himself sets out.

He identifies three potential solutions to the "tragedy of the commons": moral exhortation, privatisation and "mutual coercion mutually agreed upon". The first of these he rejects out of hand as ineffective, the second is his preferred option—when the nature of the particular commons makes this possible— while the third is a fall-back option when it is not.

While we share Hardin's assessment of the efficacy of moral exhortation as a means of solving the tragedy, we do not do so for precisely the same reasons. For him moral argument is always a kind of a sham. We are, he tells us, really being given two different messages by those who would look to moralistic solutions to problems of this nature. The first is that we should be

93

good people who should do the right thing—and it is, after all, wrong to over-exploit the commons—while the second, hidden, message is that we would have to be fools to obey this advice. But we do not have to be quite this cynical to draw the same conclusion.

The danger in Hardin's position is that his attack on "moralism" can too easily be translated into an attack on "morality" itself, and this would be self-defeating. The point is that any set of proposals for political action must ultimately rest on some ethical and moral foundations. What is always implicit in the ultimate political question, as Lenin put it, of "what is to be done?", is the ethical issue of "what *should* be done?". This is as true for Hardin as it is for anyone else who enters political debate. His reasons for wanting to solve the tragedy of the commons in the first place are clearly, if implicitly, ethical in character: he values the environment and does not wish it to be destroyed, and he is concerned with the potential damage to humans which would result from such destruction. That is, he largely shares the kind of moral humanism which also underlies our own position. If his rejection of moral exhortation leads to a rejection of morality itself then he has undermined his own argument.

Moreover, it is clear that moral arguments can be powerful, if not absolutely decisive, weapons in political debate. Consider, for example, the campaign against slavery in Europe and the United States. However cynical we may be about the ultimate reasons for its abolition, there is little doubt that the political support which led to this outcome was largely fuelled by the moral repugnance which so many in the population felt towards that pernicious institution. And much the same can be said of many broad social movements, including environmentalism itself. While we reject the particular moral formulations of some environmental writers, we cannot deny that the political strength of this movement owes much to the kind of moral disgust which so many feel at the way we have treated our world and ourselves.

And while we might agree that moral exhortation, in itself, would be ineffective in providing a solution to the tragedy, it does not follow that the creation of a particular kind of moral and ethical community will not be a part of any such solution. Indeed, if we return to a consideration of the kind of medieval communities with which we began the argument, it is obvious that the existence of a strong, and constantly reinforced, communal ethic and moral system was a significant factor in maintaining those communities against the forces which might have torn them apart. These, after all, were face to face societies, where an individual's actions were largely known of, and judged, by others. In such situations the desire to be respected by one's peers is a powerful motivating force. In fact, it is interesting to note, in this context, that many of the "punishments" for transgressing the rules found in Ostrom's analysis of "common resource regimes" are token rather than punitive. The real punishment is to be caught.

Nevertheless, a purely moralistic solution to solving the tragedy of the commons is no solution at all. Rather than being the primary means to solving the problem, the development of a strong moral commitment to the preservation of commons is more important as a potential outcome of such a solution—an outcome which will do much to maintain and support the solution, but not one which can be given much weight at the beginning of the process.[1] This is not because few of us now live in face-to-face communities, for even in such circumstances a purely moralistic approach is unlikely to work, except for a community made up exclusively of saints, and these are few and far between.

Consider the kind of community which Hardin has described (not because this represents historical reality, but as an analytic device). And add that we are not so cynical about human nature as Hardin. So, in such a situation it may well be the case that the great majority of people are moral and do have a commitment to the preservation of the commons. But even if this is the case, if it does not go beyond such a moral commitment, then the commons are under threat. This is because of the inherent fragility of systems of self-regulation. If adherence to the kind of practices which are required to maintain and enhance the fertility of commons remains purely voluntary, supported only by moral concerns, then there is always the temptation to break the rules in order to further one's own self-interest. And even in a highly moral community someone is likely to do this—to graze more than their fair share of beasts, and to do less than their fair share to maintain fertility—and to profit thereby. At this point the rot has already set in, for other herders must now reconsider their own position. And some, seeing another profit, and at their expense, will also override their own moral scruples—putting further pressure on those remaining true to their moral principles. A kind of vicious downward spiral has been created, and soon the two great catch-cries of moral breakdown—"but everyone else is doing it" and "if I don't do it then someone else will"—come into play. Eventually it is the few who do remain morally responsible who are marginalised, and who look increasingly foolish. After all, everybody else *is* doing it. Nietzsche put the point succinctly when he wrote that morality itself is in danger of dissolution when the concept of the "good person" moves too close to the concept of "stupid" or "foolish" person. For the tragedy of the commons to occur people do not have to be essentially amoral or immoral, they simply have to have the fundamental human desire not to act the fool so that others may profit where, because of their own virtue, they do not.

The lesson is that moral regimes must have some kind of institutional support if they are not to be relegated, and rapidly, to the scrap-heap of history (and every church which has survived for any length of time beyond the demise of a first charismatic leader has recognised this). The only question is: what type of institutional support?

The first, and particularly familiar, approach which Hardin suggests is privatisation. We divide the commons among the various farmers, and support that ownership through the legal institutions which uphold private property rights. Each farmer now has an interest in preserving the fertility of his or her land, and the tragedy of general degradation does not occur. In a sense, both the benefits and the costs of land use have been internalised, and none can profit at the expense of others. The morality of communal ownership is replaced by a morality of private ownership and, most importantly, this is supported by legal institutions which not only detect and punish transgressors, but by doing so help to bring the demands of the "moral" and the "rational" into closer alignment.

At first glance, and ignoring for the moment those commons—like the air—where privatisation might appear to be impractical, this does seem to solve the problem. However, on further reflection, a host of difficulties arise. Indeed, far from solving the problem the wholesale privatisation of environmental commons is more likely to exacerbate it. Rather than preventing degradation, privatisation can tend to strengthen the forces which have already led us too far in that direction. Again, we will return to the original example to make the point.

If we take Hardin to be describing a kind of peasant society then his logic does make some superficial sense. After all, in such societies people are tied to the land and their survival and well-being are dependant upon it. To allow your land to lose its fertility and become degraded is to put yourself, and your descendants, at risk. The natural, because overwhelmingly rational, ethic in such societies is one of stewardship: to pass on the land in better condition than it came to you. To care for the land, to improve it and increase its fertility, is the means to improve your own lot in life. But it is precisely these kinds of societies where systems of common ownership actually worked—where the tragedy of the commons did not occur. In fact, it is in these kinds of societies where the system of the common lands evolved and, as we pointed out in the last chapter, for good reasons. Privatisation, in such situations, is not only unnecessary, it also involves a positive loss to the communities involved (as it frequently did when the enclosures were enforced).

The situation in a highly commercialised, and decidedly non-peasant world, is very different. Here it will often be the case that the tendency of privatisation is to accelerate environmental degradation rather than to prevent it. One of the major reasons for this is the rise and increasing dominance of the so-called "managerial" class. As any number of commentators have pointed out, capitalism in the twentieth century has undergone a major transformation. Where in the nineteenth century the major critics of capitalism, like Marx and Engels, focused on the role of ownership and the "owning classes", with the rapid growth of the corporate world, and particularly multi-national, transnational and what might be called mega-corporations, the balance of economic power has shifted from owners to managers, and increasingly to "upper management". In particular, the often family-based enterprises of the late nineteenth and early twentieth centuries have frequently been replaced by extremely large conglomerations where ownership, through share holdings, is widely distributed, and the power of many individual shareholders is minuscule in comparison to that of upper management. One of the primary results of this, magnified by the operations of largely unrestricted capital markets, has been a growing emphasis on short-term profit making. Again, one of the best ways to illustrate this is through the example of agriculture.

The world of the peasant is timeless, in the sense that it is tradition bound. One does not clearly distinguish between the past, the present and the future, for the quite reasonable expectation is that they will all be much the same. And in such a case, as we have already pointed out, the natural tendency is towards a stewardship ethic and the development of the kind of sustainable agricultural practices which go along with this. In the transitional phase of the "family farm" the orientation has moved towards profit (and this leads to its own problems), but much of the ethic of stewardship is retained in the common desire to pass on the farm as a viable, even improved, enterprise for one's descendants. But such long-term considerations have little or no place in the fully corporatised world of modern agri-business. For, unlike the peasant or even the dedicated family farmer, modern corporate executives, and the stocks of capital they control, are highly mobile. Because of this, and because it is now common practice for the (usually very substantial) remuneration of senior management to be tied directly to annual profitability, their attitudes to land-use will tend to be very different from either the peasant or the family farmer.

For a person in this position it makes every sense to concentrate on short-term profit, even if this is at the expense of long-term viability. The capital generated in a few years of intense exploitation can readily be transferred to some new operation, while the reputation the executive gains as an efficient profit-maker forms the foundation for any potential application for some new position which may arise, either within the particular corporation or with a different one. That, in the process, the land may have been significantly degraded, is simply irrelevant—the money, and the person, have moved on.

This is an extreme example, and there is no doubt that there are many managers who have a longer-term commitment to their enterprises than this, but it is, nevertheless, the *natural* tendency in a highly privatised and corporatised world. The kind of manager who is concerned to create steady and sustainable growth will be unlikely to be able to produce the same level of profit, in any given year, as those with no such concern, and shareholders will tend to judge them on the levels of dividend they produce. Almost inevitably, in a highly competitive environment the later style will tend to win out, with its practitioners advancing to more and more powerful positions. And this is not just the case in the realm of agriculture—it applies in every area of resource usage,[2] and equally inevitably, it tends to be the environment which loses out.

Furthermore, even when managers do have a more benevolent outlook than this, the situation in which they find themselves may well prevent them from acting in appropriate ways. So for example, "family farmers" may well be aware that the kind of practices they engage in are not sustainable in the long-term, and they may wish to move to more ecologically sound forms of production, but very often this is a difficult or even impossible task. Frequently, and in order to compete, they have had to borrow significant amounts—for machinery, equipment and land—and the interest payments must be met if the banks are not to foreclose. Again, this means that it is *this* years profits which count. There is a tendency, then, toward the development of a "one big crop" syndrome: the attempt to gain the kind of short-term profit which might allow them to reduce their debt substantially. And even if they are successful in this (and the "one big crop" rarely comes), the transition to, say, organic systems of farming, will not only be expensive, but will probably involve some initial loss of production. The pressure is always to remain with existing, even if unsustainable, practices.

The general point is that in the privatised world of market competition, even the most well-intentioned can be subject to a range of external forces which prevent them from operating in ecologically sound ways. This is as true of manufacturing as it is of mining, of farming or fishing or forestry, in a competitive market it is profit, and only profit, which counts, and maximisation of profit is rarely environmentally benign—particularly when you must compete with those who have few, if any scruples in this area.

Even apart from these tendencies, privatisation, as an attempted solution to the tragedy of the commons, only really deals with half the problem. For even in the best possible case, of dedicated family farmers who have now internalised their own costs and have a long-term commitment to maintaining and improving the fertility of their lands, there is still always the possibility for other kinds of externalities to come into play. So, for example, while I may now be dedicated to the maintenance of *my* land, I have no such commitment to *yours* (which was at least possible when it was *ours*). If my farming practices lead, say, to the excessive run-off of nutrients or chemicals, which pollutes the stream which your cattle rely on, this is not part of my problem. Indeed, it may well be that I am now more unconcerned about potential pollution of a stream which previously, as part of a commons, I had access to, but now no longer do. Privatisation in one area may well exacerbate the pressures on those commons which do remain, particularly when they are difficult to privatise themselves.

Finally, apart from such practical problems, there are a number of political and ideological concerns which any environmentalist should have about the consequences of privatisation of commons as a general policy. Firstly, privatisation involves the removal of resources from public hands to private hands, from the community to the market. If it is a genuine privatisation then this always involves the possibility of sale and resale. That is, the resource is now controlled as a business. Such a process can only strengthen what is called the "business sector" and, around the world, it is this sector which has typically been most hostile to the proposals put forward by green groups. In effect, this approach to dealing with environmental problems will likely boost those who, traditionally, have been least likely to show any genuine commitment to the environmental cause. It is rarely good politics to hand power to your opponents. Secondly, privatisation necessarily involves an extension of the market and market relations. And the market, by its very nature, encourages a certain kind of mentality: the mentality of the self-interested utility maximiser of classical economic theory. But one way to read the tragedy of the commons is as precisely the tragedy of this kind of mentality. Hardin's herdsmen are utility maximisers who, by simply following their own (apparent) self-interest, create disaster for all. To encourage that mentality, and the free market ideology which goes with it, is not, ultimately, to solve tragedies of the commons, but to reinforce the conditions which lead to them.

If we have little faith in privatisation as a means to solve the tragedy of the commons, what then of Hardin's other suggestion: "mutual coercion mutually agreed upon"? Here much depends on how this phrase is interpreted, and Hardin has little to say on this.

However, the most obvious reading is that Hardin is presenting us with what might be called a "Hobbesian" solution. This follows from his radical attack on morality. Because, for Hardin, morality is always just a kind of veneer used to disguise the baser self-interest which really drives how people behave, it would seem that, like Hobbes, he has to look to some external authority as a means of controlling people's tendency to act in ultimately destructive ways. It is not just that we cannot always trust people to act correctly, but that we can never do so. Hence his emphasis on "coercion". While he adds the rider that there should be "mutual agreement" to this, it is a secondary consideration. The "mutual agreement" is to be coerced, and this, it seems, is the end of the matter. After we have created the instruments of control they are there to do precisely that: control us. It is to the strong and benevolent state which we must look if we are ultimately to solve the tragedy of the commons.

We suspect that this was an unpalatable conclusion for Hardin to draw, which is why he, and many of his interpreters place so much emphasis on the supposed solution of wholesale privatisation. For the model which most readily comes to mind is the kind of state socialism which characterised the old USSR and Eastern Bloc countries. When the underlying reality of politics is conceived of as a kind of war—whether this is Hobbes' "war of all against all" in his "state of nature", the kind of "class warfare" suggested by more radical socialists, or the war between "nations" or "races" described by fascists and Nazis—then authoritarian solutions seem to be the only possibilities. But while the total mobilisation and clear lines of authority of a war based approach to problem solving may have some short-term successes, it is particularly unstable in the long term.

A brief glance at the history of the old USSR should be enough to make the case. Here we have a polity founded by radicals, perceived by themselves and others, as absolutely dedicated to the communist ideal—a society of total equality based on the principle "from each according to ability, to each according to need". And it is possible to point to some great achievements of the regime which developed. They not only survived a debilitating civil war, and a massively destructive world war but, in a period of some fifty years, industrialised what had essentially been an agricultural society, significantly raised the standards of living of the people, and developed enviable systems in the public provision of health, education and welfare. Yet it is clear that the fundamental ideals which fuelled the revolutionary passion of the original Bolsheviks were betrayed in the process. The upper echelons of the party and bureaucracy lived lives of privilege and hypocrisy beyond the dreams of ordinary citizens, and it was at least partly the resentment of this which ultimately helped to undermine the system. Furthermore, the area of the environment was one of their greatest failures. One example is instructive enough.

In the late 1950s the government of the Union of Soviet Socialist Republics, aiming for economic development to match that of the "Free World", decided on the basis of "expert opinion" that Kazakstan was ideally suited to become the "cotton bowl" of the nation. Using the latest technological developments the two rivers feeding the Aral Sea, the Amu Dar`ya and the Syr Dar`ya were diverted to provide irrigation for the massive cotton crops which extended across a broad belt over 200 miles wide. Momentarily a "success", it soon became clear that the effort to increase agricultural productivity through sophisticated technological strategies aimed at reshaping and exploiting nature actually ushered in a disaster of massive, if local, scale. In part the disaster was direct: the cotton bowl soon became entirely unproductive for any kind of agricultural production. A Soviet scientist in the *New Scientist* travelling across the plain recently reported "what appeared to be a snow-covered plain stretching to the horizon without a sign of life." The irrigation efforts boosted productivity for a while, but soon salinisation and waterlogging drastically reduced yields, while an indirect consequence—the loss of 56% of the surface area of the Aral Sea, and 75% of its volume—saw the wind spread huge amounts of salt from the exposed sea bed, and pesticides from cotton spraying onto the previously fertile plain, and into the environment of the local population with resulting large scale health problems. More than this, the effort at cotton production effectively wiped out the previously vibrant and productive fishing industry centred on the Aral Sea. Fish yields dropped from around 50,000 tons annually to zero, obliterating in the process 60,000 jobs. Finally, the retreat of the Aral Sea and loss of vegetation cover has seen the local climate change for the worse, with precipitation reduced, an increase in average temperature, and furious dust storms.

It is clear that even though the government well knew of the kind of damage to their people and their land occurring because of their approach to industrial development and resource exploitation, it was expedient to maintain it, and they did. As a result some of the worst pollution in the world, and some of the largest potential environmental disasters, can be found in those countries which once made up the old USSR. If nothing else this should suggest that authoritarianism is no friend of environmentalism.

Again, the general logic behind this process is clear enough. It is best summed up in Lord Acton's dictum: "power corrupts, and absolute power corrupts absolutely." Even those most dedicated to a cause can change over time, particularly if they have much to gain from it, and while there are some who will remain pure, what of those who follow them? Authoritarian regimes are always susceptible to internal corruption—if there is any lesson of history it is this. And this is the case even when that authority is limited to particular areas, if it is the kind of unrestrained authority promoted by Hobbes (and implicitly, we would suggest, by Hardin).

But there is another way Hardin's missive might be interpreted, although both the language and the form must be altered. Rather than "mutual coercion, mutually agreed upon", we would suggest "common agreement to mutual restraint". This may seem a mere linguistic change, but it is one which gives us a different emphasis and image. For now the underlying image of politics is not of a "war of all against all" where we can only rely on coercion to save us, but an image of mutual cooperation which we might gladly accept. In terms of political theory the difference here is the difference between Hobbes and Locke, and it is to this later theorist which we now turn.

In order to understand fully the kind of political theory developed by John Locke, and to see how it might bear on the tragedy of the commons, we need to look first of all, if only briefly, at the period in which he lived. Here there are two major points to be made. The first is that the seventeenth century, when he lived and worked, was a time of great political turmoil. In Britain there was a major civil war—the Stuart monarchs were deposed, then eventually restored, only to be deposed again. The long struggle between Parliament and the Monarchy came to a head in the "Glorious Revolution" of 1688, which set the foundations for the modern British system of government. It was, in short, a period of political chaos, and in such times theorists tend to ask big questions. The second is that this is also the period when the European colonisation of North America began to expand at a rapid rate. The possibilities this presented—of new beginnings in a "New World"—lent a kind of optimism to people like Locke, and this was also reflected in his political thought, and profoundly influenced his conception of both the "state of nature" and the "social contract".

The big question that Locke asked was "what are governments for?" And, in order to answer this he relied on what we would now call a "thought experiment": his idea of the "state of nature". Here we are asked to imagine what social existence would be like if there were no government—if we were all autonomous individuals with no external authorities to control us. But where for Hobbes this would be the horror of a constant "war of all against all" where "the lives of men would be poor, nasty, brutish and short", Locke paints a far more idyllic scene. In such a situation, he suggests, we would not be without morality or sociability. These are a part of our nature as human beings, not simply a product of governance. The "state of nature", then, would be a realm of freedom, where everyone would be able to create their own property by "mixing their labour with the land"—a society of independent yeoman farmers. But in this potential Garden of Eden serpents await. In particular, Locke argues, there would be two intractable problems which would arise: the problems of justice and security.

The problem of justice arises in the state of nature because we must all be judges in our own cases. If justice is to be served, in such a situation, then we, as individuals, must decide what is just, and act to enforce this. And this is especially the case when we are directly involved. If we believe that we have been treated unjustly or harmed by another then it is up to *us* to do something about it. And the problem arises because of the natural tendency to be partial when we are judging in our own cases: we tend to exaggerate the harms done to us, and underestimate the harms we do to others—and the following kind of scenario unfolds all too easily. You inadvertently kill one of my stock and I demand compensation. But the amount of compensation I ask for seems excessive to you and, insulted, you refuse to pay it. This makes me angry, and I demand in a louder voice and make threats. This makes you very angry, and you push me, and I punch you, and then we both draw swords. We have taken the first footstep on the path to vendetta politics, and generations later our descendants are still killing each other. Even though the cause of the original dispute may be trivial, or even forgotten, our very sense of justice locks us into a vicious spiral of reprisal and counter-reprisal and, almost invariably, the innocent are drawn into this.[3] In seeking justice we have created a situation which leads directly to injustice.

The problem of personal security has a similar form (and one which should be particularly familiar in the modern world). Again, we tend to be partial in our own cases—to trust ourselves more that we trust others. So, even though you and I might be on quite amicable terms, when I notice that your knife is considerably larger than mine—which would give you the advantage if we did have a dispute—I become nervous and, purely for personal security, buy a sword. But, even though you have no reason to believe that I have any evil intention towards you, you are now nervous, and buy a sword and some armour. Soon we are both buying spears and crossbows, and so on. Another vicious spiral—an arms race—has been set in motion and, sooner or later, the option of a pre-emptive strike becomes increasingly attractive to one or other of us. In trying to ensure our personal security, we create the conditions which undermine it.

The first thing to note here is that both of these situations have precisely the same *form* as the tragedy of the commons. One way to sum this up is to say that they are all tragedies of independent action in conditions of scarcity. If the commons were infinite then it would not matter how many extra beasts we placed on them. In the same way, if justice was automatic—a law of nature—or if we were all invulnerable to attack, then the problems of injustice or personal insecurity would also not arise. It is precisely because these things are in short supply that our fully independent attempts to attain them are doomed to failure. And the solution to these kinds of problems also have the same form (although the details may vary considerably). The only way we can solve these problems, indeed the only way in which we can achieve what we wanted in the first place, is if we give up our right to independent action in these arenas for a system of collectively ordered action. In effect, we create a government which, in turn, creates agencies—like the courts and the police force—to regulate these areas of our lives.

This, then, is Locke's notion of the "social contract". We agree with each other to give up our right to independent action in a particular area if others will also do the same. And here there is the possibility of creating virtuous rather than vicious cycles, for I am more likely to uphold the law if I am confident that you will also do so. In the situation of the agricultural commons, once we have agreed to regulate its use, then it now becomes rational for me to co-operate with you to maintain and enhance its fertility, for in this way we will both benefit. Furthermore, while we may have appeared to have given something up—our right to independent action—we have actually gained. For what *use* are the rights to enforce personal justice, or ensure our personal security, or to use the commons as we please, if the *result* is injustice, insecurity, or the destruction of those very commons? In being part of a social contract we achieve the ends which we originally sought.

In effect, for Locke (as for Greg in our earlier example), this is the rationale for Government—to solve these kinds of problems. This is what politics is, or at least should be, about. Furthermore, this is *all* that it should be about. It is at this point that Locke diverges so markedly from Hobbes, who had insisted that our involvement in a social contract requires that we surrender all our rights to some centralised Leviathan. In contrast, a Lockean position insists that we only give up some of our rights of independent action to Government, and only in so far as Government then acts to ensure those rights. Government, in effect, does not reduce our rights, it is the means by which we make them useful and effective. This is the radical side of Locke. For he insists that if the government infringes the rights we retain—and particularly the rights to Life, Liberty and Property—then we have the right, even the duty, to rebel. So, if government does not act in the way it should, then we should remove it—it has lost its legitimacy. This is a notion of *limited* and *constitutional* government. And, if we accept that this style of government is the best means of solving tragedies of the commons, then this has a number of major implications for a genuinely Green politics.

The first is that Environmentalism does not require the development of some new style of politics, it is perfectly consistent with the liberal-democratic tradition of western society. Locke, after all, was a highly influential political thinker—not only because of his defence of Parliament against monarchical power in the British system, but even more obviously in his direct influence on the founders of the American political system (you need to do little more than glance at the Declaration of Independence or the U.S. Constitution to make that point). If anything, an environmental politics requires us to uncover, and perhaps recover, some of the very foundations of our own political systems which have not so much been repudiated as increasingly forgotten in the foreground obsessions of much modern liberal-democratic politics.

There is a considerable irony here, for many of the developments which, we would argue, are undermining these very foundations have, themselves, been justified in seemingly Lockean terms. In particular, the many arguments for "smaller" or "minimalist" styles of government—put forward by libertarians like Robert Nozick for example—have a distinctly "Lockean" flavour to them—particularly in their emphasis on "natural rights". But we have suggested, right from the beginnings of this argument, that green politics cannot help but involve a significant extension of the regulatory powers of government. How can these, apparently contradictory, conclusions be drawn from the same source? In Chapter Four we located the problem in terms of a confusion or ignorance of the importance of the foreground/background distinction, but we did not give an account there of the source of this mistake. To provide this we need to take a closer look at the differences between Locke's world and our world, and particularly at the nature of "scarcity" in these contexts.

Although it is rarely mentioned explicitly, the problem of scarcity is fundamental to virtually all attempts to theorise about politics. Indeed, some theorists go so far as to identify this as the central issue of political life. Harold Lasswell,[4] for example, actually defines politics in terms of "who gets what, when, and how". And, apart from some classical conservative exceptions, this problem is typically solved in the major ideological formulations by relying on some notion of abundance. This is most obvious in classical Marxism. For Marx it is the historical role of the capitalist classes, through their constant revolutionising of the means of production, to unleash those enormous productive powers which, in the coming communist society, will be more than enough to provide for all, particularly since the false wants created by the commodity fetishism of capitalism will no longer exist. In this general image he, perhaps suprisingly, shares a great deal with those liberal-capitalist theorists who see economic growth as the solution to the problem of scarcity. For these theorists it is the constant economic growth produced by the dynamism of the free enterprise system which allows a compromise between equity and efficiency: our shares of the cake may be very unequal, but as long as the cake itself is expanding it does not matter. We are all better off.

The thing to note about these kinds of theories is that they focus on scarcity only in terms of the products of human effort. To draw on a distinction we made in an earlier chapter, they are concerned with scarcities in the *foreground* of human existence. Indeed, amongst the major social theorists it is only Malthus who considers the issue of scarcities in the *background*—in those basic resources on which all wealth is built. In our view in most modern political theory the problem of scarcity in the foreground is solved only by the assumption of abundance in the background. Locke falls clearly into this category.

This becomes most apparent when we examine his theory of property. The idea of "property" is one of the central themes of Locke's political theory, so much so that some commentators[5] identify it as the fundamental notion which drives the rest of his argument. For Locke we gain the right to the ownership of property by mixing our labour with the land. The image is clear enough: the yeoman farmer encloses an area of wilderness, clears it and farms it. It is the labour involved which transforms the area, and what was once unproductive, and therefore in a sense worthless, is now productive and of significant worth. So, at least in the original acquisition of property, we put something of ourselves—our labour—into the land, and this is what gives it value. For Locke, then, we own property in the same way that we own ourselves, because its value arises because we have mixed something of ourselves with it. Our ownership of property, in this view, is absolute—we have the right to do with it as we will, and to pass it on to whomever we choose. It is this side of Locke which has typically been taken up by a number of radical libertarian theorists and used to justify notions of the "minimal" state.

However, what these same theorists either forget, or choose to ignore, is that Locke's justification for the ownership of property is not, itself, absolute. For while we have the right to create property by mixing our labour with the land, we can only do so if we "leave enough, and good enough, for others". This is Locke's *proviso*. And, for Locke, this is no mere addendum to be puzzled at (as it is for some of his followers), it follows directly from his conception of human rights. For Locke, we all have rights, and we all have equal rights, because we are all, equally, God's creatures. We have the right to acquire property because God made the world for our use. But, again, the world was made for all of us, and equally. So, our right to acquire property, like all our other rights, only holds to the extent that we do not infringe on the same rights which are held by others. If we do not "leave enough, and good enough" then this is not the case—we have gained our property at the expense of other people's ability to do so. And, as in all other cases where the exercise of *my* rights has the potential to undermine *your* rights there is a role, indeed a necessity, for governance.

But the right to gain, use and enjoy property in an unrestricted and ungoverned way, presented no problem for those living in Locke's world. It was, after all (if only from a strictly Eurocentric perspective), a world in which there was, manifestly, enough and good enough which could be left for others. This was particularly obvious in North America (where Lockean theory sunk its deepest roots). For the next two hundred years the adage "go west young man" actually made some sense—there was fertile land to be gained just beyond the frontier. In today's world, if we follow the same advice, then we simply end up in Los Angeles (or in our case, Perth). The abundance on which the Lockean case for non-interference and non-regulation rests no longer exists.

And this is not only the case in respect to land. In the modern, industrialised world the ownership of capital is of far greater economic significance than the ownership of land, and it might be argued that, unlike the land, capital is an infinite resource—it is, after all, created, not simply discovered. However, what the environmental evidence now indicates is that the unrestrained use of capital is also running into problems of scarcity which were not envisaged in earlier ages. It is not just that we are running out of potentially productive land, but clean air and water as well as a whole variety of mineral and biotic resources are increasingly difficult to secure. While the productive capacity of "developed" societies is easily enough to provide their citizens with much more than just their basic needs, the broad environment on which this wealth is ultimately built is increasingly under threat. The problem of scarcity has moved from the foreground to the background. The "open commons" in environmental goods which prevailed must be replaced by "social commons" if tragedy is not to strike us all.

But, as this analysis has shown, this situation does not require us to develop some totally new theory of government but simply to re-read and re-assess what we already have. A political theory which, in a world dominated by agriculture and blessed with an open frontier, led to visions of a minimal state and *laissez faire* economics, now leads us in different directions, but the fundamentals remain the same. It is the situation which has changed, not the theory. Indeed, it may well be that such a re-reading and re-assessment will lead us to re-capture some of those fundamentals—the ideals of human dignity and freedom on which liberal-democratic theory was founded. These, after all, are what politics in our kind of society is supposed to be about, even though many of us, including many of our politicians, may have forgotten this.

The solution to the "tragedy of the commons" is to be found in politics. But it must be a politics which is genuinely conceived—as an expression of human rights in a process of cooperation for the attainment of common goods—not the kind of power-broking which passes for politics in what are essentially authoritarian regimes. But the immediate objection to this is that it might well require an extension of government, and isn't this, as Hayek put it, "the road to serfdom"? Isn't the extension of government the extension of authority, and isn't this equivalent to the kind of authoritarianism we have already rejected? It is to this issue which we will now turn.

Notes

1   This is the same kind of error made by many contemporary "communitarian" theorists. Their argument can be summed up as "if only people were more moral then things might be better", but it is truer to say that "if only things were better then people might be more moral".

2   In fact, it applies even more widely than this—to what might be called the "meta-resources" of enterprises themselves. Hence the success of "corporate raiders". But a further investigation of this would lead us away from the particular issues which are of concern here.

3   For a striking account of such a feud and its disastrous logic, see Mark Twain, *Life on the Mississippi*, Chapter XXVL, "Under Fire", (Harmondsworth: Penguin, 1986).

4   Harold Lasswell, *Politics: Who Gets What, When, How*, (New York: Meridian, 1972).

5   See, for example, C. B. MacPherson, *The Political Theory of Possessive Individualism*, (Oxford: Clarendon Press, 1962).

7 Political Ecology and Government

Any serious attempt to deal with the kind of environmental problems which face our world will certainly involve an expansion of government authority, not only domestically but internationally. Even in those cases where market mechanisms might be used to help solve particular problems (in say, a trade in water user's licences) such a market itself exists only in the context of some overall system of government regulation. And there are many other cases where direct regulation, or even state ownership will be required. Certain kinds of activities will have to be banned and others strictly controlled. All of this will involve an expansion of the powers of the state, because in our world it is only states, at the level of the modern nation-state, which have the necessary authority, legitimacy and degree of sovereignty to achieve what is required. This for many commentators, as we have already pointed out, raises the spectre of "Big", and therefore "Authoritarian", government. And it might be argued that, while we have explicitly rejected authoritarian approaches to environmentalism, authoritarianism remains implicit in the kinds of solutions we advocate. While we can understand why such a charge might be laid, particularly in the context of much of modern political rhetoric, it rests on a misunderstanding of the nature and point of that ecological conception of politics we have developed. In particular it rests on a common misunderstanding of the relationship between "authority", "authoritarianism" and "liberty". To understand why such a misunderstanding occurs, and so often, we need to consider some aspects of the history of the twentieth century.

By any measure the twentieth century has been a tumultuous period in human existence—a time of rapid and continuing change. On the one hand it has seen massive industrial, economic and technological developments which have significantly improved standards of living for much of the world's population (although not by any means all); on the other, we have witnessed a period of revolution and counter-revolution, of the breakdown of mighty empires and the rise of anti-colonial regimes, of depression and economic boom. And above all, the twentieth century has been a time of small and large scale warfare—most notably the First and Second World Wars but, equally significantly, over forty years of paranoia known as the Cold War. These events have not only massively re-shaped the political map of the world they have had an equal effect on our common political consciousness. In particular, they have had a very significant effect on the way we typically divide up the political world.

For much of the last half of the century—in the long period since the end of the second world war to the fall of the USSR—the most fundamental of these divides was between the "liberal democracies" of the West and the "people's democracies" of the east. This was a divide which affected all countries and all peoples, even those who did not fit easily into one or other of these camps. For while it was a "cold" war it had numerous "hot" spots— in Latin America, Africa, the Middle East and, most clearly and directly, in Asia. And, in some readings at least,[1] the final outcome of the struggle between these two ways of political organisation and ideology has been the culmination of the triumph of the West. It triumphed first against the monarchical autocracies of Central and Eastern Europe, secondly against the militaristic dictatorships of Nazi Germany, Fascist Italy and Imperial Japan, and finally against the ideological totalitarianism of Communism. But in the process, we shall argue, it also transformed itself, and particularly its understanding of itself—its self-definition.

There were a number of elements involved in this process, but possibly the most important was concerned with our perception of the "other". Societies and political systems, as much as individuals, tend to define themselves not only in terms of what they are but, just as importantly, in terms of what they are not. And when one is involved in a long struggle, when the focus is always on the enemy, the second of these tendencies can easily overwhelm the first. Something of this kind appears to have happened, and in a way which has had a significant impact on how we perceive our own society. We, after all, were the "free world", to be contrasted with the (implicitly "unfree") "communist bloc". And the distinction between these revolved around two broad categories: the political and the economic.

At a political level a distinction was made between "liberal" and "authoritarian" approaches to politics. At least nominally the West had a system which upheld basic political rights, had relatively free and fair elections, and worked by the "rule of law". We had rights to freedom of speech and association—to speak our minds and to organise together for political purposes—our electoral systems gave us a genuine opportunity to change our governments, and our judiciary was largely free of direct political control.

These ideals were not always lived up to, but there was, nevertheless, a clear difference between this style of government and the "one party" systems of the East. There it could often be dangerous to speak one's mind about political matters or to create non-party organisations, elections could only return the existing government—perhaps with a few changed faces—and the courts were little more than instruments of direct political control. Although not always as harshly totalitarian as they were painted in the West, in contrast to liberal political systems they were highly authoritarian, centralised and intrusive regimes. And this lack of freedom carried over to the economic realm. The West had a capitalist form of economic organisation, at least theoretically based on a "free market" where the individual choices of suppliers and consumers drove economic development. The East, in direct contrast, had "command" economies where, again at least in theory, economic development was based on centralised government planning, ownership and control.

As the cold war progressed these kinds of features came increasingly to be perceived as natural clusters. Thus, the "small" government and capitalist economic organisation of the West became associated with "freedom", while the "big" government and highly regulated economies of the East became equated with authoritarianism. This was a natural association, and one constantly reinforced in the ideological battles of the cold war, but it reflects the contingency of a particular history, not a theoretical or even practical necessity. Even more, it involves a denial, or at the very least a forgetting, of the origins of the "free" liberal-democratic regimes.

For the movements which ultimately led to the creation of the modern "western" styles of government, as well as the ideologies on which they were based, did not begin in opposition to "big" government at all, they developed in opposition to authoritarian government—and these are quite different things. If we were to characterise the "eastern" systems as "elephant" governments—crushing the freedom from their people—then the regimes which initially spawned a liberal opposition might be called "wolverine" governments: small, but extremely nasty. It was not so much that such regimes "crushed" people's freedoms as "ripped them to shreds" (almost literally)—at least if they happened to get in the way. These were the absolute monarchies, epitomised in the regimes of Henry VIII in Britain and Louis XIV in France.

The thing to note about these regimes is that, by today's standards, they were extremely "small" forms of government which had virtually nothing to do with many of the functions which we associate with modern nation-states. They were not, except in the most marginal ways, concerned with things like health, education or welfare—these were local issues, dealt with at a local level—and their "economic management" was almost entirely directed at the raising of revenue and maintaining the privileges of the aristocratic elites. While they were concerned to "uphold the law" most of this was done by local officials who were virtually autonomous. Certainly there was nothing like the developed and extensive policing and legal systems which we have today, and those that did exist were military in character. For these were, in essence, military regimes. Their power derived from their control of military might, and their primary purpose was to maintain and expand that might. Even the systems of land ownership were based on the obligation to raise revenue and troops for the King, and the aristocratic titles which went with such ownership were equivalent to military ranks in the armies of the Kingdom.

While these regimes were not large in any sense of the word, they were arbitrary, and vicious. The monarchs were, effectively, above the law—indeed, they *were* the law—and any opposition to them was treated in the harshest ways imaginable. It was in the context of such regimes that liberal ideas and movements developed, to be ultimately expressed in the triumph of Parliament over the Monarchy in Britain and in the bloody revolution in France. And it is also this context which makes the fundamental tenets of liberal democratic regimes explicable—the insistence on the fundamental moral equality (and, therefore, rights) of *all* people, and on the rule of Law, not of men. Liberalism, after all, grew in opposition to regimes which were explicitly hierarchical— where particular rights and obligations were attached to particular social positions—and where rule could become arbitrary at any time—dependent on the whims of a single individual.

So, at the very least, we must recognise that there is no necessary connection between the size of government and its authoritarian or non-authoritarian character. It is perfectly possible to have "big" governments which uphold liberal-democratic principles and "small" governments which are highly authoritarian. Indeed, there are many examples to be found in today's world. Compare, for example, the "social democracies" of Northern Europe with any of the "military" regimes of the "third world". There is also some evidence—such as incarceration rates—to suggest that, as western governments "downsized" during the 1980s and 90s, they actually became more, rather than less, authoritarian in character.

Nor is there any necessary connection between political liberalism and economic capitalism. We need to look no further than the economies of Asia to make that point. In regimes such as Singapore, South Korea and increasingly China, capitalist forms of economic organisation have mixed quite happily with forms of political authoritarianism. At the same time one can point to countries like Sweden where, in the mid 1980s, something over 60% of GDP was a product of government activity, and yet which were not notably authoritarian in character. So, by any empirical measure, the equation of "authoritarianism" with "big" governments with a high degree of economic control, and freedom with "small" government and *laissez faire* economics, simply cannot be justified. Yet, this kind of connection is now pervasive at the level of economic and political theory and ideology.

This was not always the case, particularly if we go back to the beginnings of the cold war, where the "dominant wisdom" was quite different. The post-war period spawned a peculiar group of politicians and bureaucrats. Their major formative experiences were the Great Depression and the Second World War. The first had taught them of the human misery and political dangers associated with high and persistent levels of unemployment, while the second—with its enormous increase in productive capacity and virtual elimination of unemployment in the West as well as the successful conclusion of the war—had given them faith in the abilities of government to effectively cope with massive difficulties. Their spiritual leader was John Maynard Keynes, the Cambridge economist whose theories on the necessity of government intervention to prevent a "high unemployment equilibrium" they now (at least partially) began to put into practice. In the period of their dominance they not only ushered in the "long boom" of the 1950s and 1960s, where virtually full employment was the norm, but also created the modern "welfare" state, which gave some hope to those who, for one reason or other, did not share in the benefits which accrued to the rest of the population.

And Keynes, while he has sometimes been labelled a "social democrat", can quite clearly be placed in the long tradition of British liberalism. This was a liberalism which not only had to cope with a frontier which, since the American revolution, was not quite so accessible, but also with the effects of an emerging industrial society. Where in America, with its constantly expanding frontier, the Lockean vision of a nation of yeoman farmers jealously protective of their "natural rights" and ruled in only minimal ways, continued to make real sense, right up until the beginnings of the twentieth century, this was not the case in much of Europe—and particularly in Britain. There the enclosure movement was increasingly driving the peasantry from the land and into the cities, where the burgeoning "industrial revolution" transformed them into factory workers—the industrial proletariat championed in the emerging socialist ideologies. British liberalism, therefore, had to deal with new conditions and new ideas in a way in which its American counterpart largely did not. This transformed liberal approaches to politics and political thinking in a number of important ways.

While the central tenet of Locke's liberalism—the underlying moral equality of all humans—remained as a fundamental element of liberal thought, other aspects were modified or discarded. Among the first, and most significant, of these changes was a rejection of the Lockean notion of "absolute natural rights". Rights conceived in this way were, as Jeremy Bentham thundered, "nonsense on stilts". What counted, rather, were the rights embedded in Law, and it was to the reform of the Law, in light of the principle of "the greatest happiness of the greatest number", to which he turned his attention. This strict utilitarianism was later to be modified by John Stuart Mill who saw liberty, and the moral autonomy it both allowed and encouraged, as "goods" to be sought in their own right, above and beyond any immediate happiness they might bring. And it was Mill who became increasingly doubtful of the ability of a *laissez faire* economic system to create the kinds of conditions which would allow the great majority of people to attain such "goods" in any meaningful way. This doubt was taken up and developed by T. H. Green in his distinction between *negative* and *positive* freedom.[2]

Negative freedom, as he pointed out, means simply to be left alone—to be able to do what one wants to do without outside interference or regulation. It was this understanding which had been (and still, very often, is) championed by liberal theorists. But, for Green, this was only half the question of liberty. For unless such freedom is matched with a significant degree of positive freedom—conceived as a positive power to do or achieve something worth doing or achieving—it means very little. What point, for instance, is there in having the right to develop our own moral consciousness without outside interference, if the circumstances which surround us effectively prevent us from doing so? In a more cynical way of making the same kind of point Rousseau had earlier remarked "both the rich man and the poor man are 'free' to sleep under bridges". And it was in the economic realm that the problems associated with a purely negative conception of freedom became most apparent.

For where the yeoman farmer, equipped with little more than a few tools and the skills acquired from a life of agriculture, and having access to a frontier where "enough and good enough" had been left, could by mixing his labour with the land, achieve a degree of economic success and the independence which went with this, the same was not nearly so clear for the majority of people in the vastly more complex world of a now industrialised society. While a few might claw their way through the ranks and achieve success, and others be born into it, the great majority—as hired workers on poor wages—were effectively relegated to a life of economic dependency. And, as Mill had noted, those who are dependent have little chance to develop their own abilities. In particular, for this is what mattered to both Mill and Green, they had little chance to develop their own moral character or to think independently, as they were always subject to the orders of others. They may have had formal freedoms, but this mattered little if they could not put these into effect.

This kind of argument had major implications for liberal views on the nature and character of government. Where earlier liberals, still fearful of the authoritarian aspects of the monarchical state, viewed government with some suspicion, and were concerned to emphasise the limits on its power, for these modern liberals the—now democratised—government had a positive role to play: not merely to protect rights, but also to act positively to help create those conditions which would allow genuine freedoms to flourish. In the kind of terminology we have used before, government was to be not only concerned with the *foreground* of political rights, but also with the social and economic *background* which made those rights meaningful. It was this positive view of government which British liberals brought into the twentieth century, which was reinforced by the experience of the Great Depression and the Second World War, and which underpinned the Keynesian "revolution" of the post-war era.

There was nothing inconsistent in this apparent transformation of liberalism. For while Green may have made the notion of "positive freedom" explicit, he really only brought out something which was already central to liberal conceptions of politics. While the emphasis of earlier liberals, like Locke, was on the question of what governments should *not* do, they nevertheless had a theory of government—they were not, after all, anarchists. And, as should be clear from our earlier analysis, the role they assigned to government was a positive one. It was not just that people required governance to solve the problems of injustice and insecurity in the state of nature, but that in solving these problems through the internalising mechanism of a social contract, government actually *creates* the possibility of both justice and security—it sets up the conditions under which these things might now be achieved. Even more, it creates these in a way which not only recognises, but aims to ensure, the underlying moral equality of all human beings. But this was also Green's project. It is not so much that the theory has changed—it has been developed rather than transformed—but that it has different consequences when applied to different circumstances. In an agricultural and frontier society it may point in the direction of a "minimal" state; in an industrial society with a closed frontier it does not. And, even more cogently, it does not point in this direction in societies threatened by environmental disaster.

Now, it must be recognised that governments concerned to promote positive freedoms can, in some cases, only achieve this through the extension of their regulatory powers. And this can mean that, in certain areas at least, they must become more authoritative—that is to say they involve some restriction of the choices available to individuals and organisations. But we should not make the simplistic assumption that "freedom", understood in any broad way, equates directly with "freedom of choice". While this equation might make some sense in certain areas of economic life—in the purchase, say, of baked beans or motor vehicles—there are many other areas where real freedom involves a certain freedom *from* choices in the foreground. Consider, for instance, driving a car. We could increase the freedom of choice involved in this activity by allowing each of us, as individuals, to decide on which side of the road we wished to drive. But only the terminally suicidal would actually wish to drive in such a situation. In what sense, then, has our freedom been extended by increasing our freedom of choice in such cases? Most of us would perceive ourselves to be considerably freer when we did not have such a choice as this to make.

The general point has already been made in our earlier analysis. The realm of negative freedom is equivalent to the *state of nature*, and there are many situations where living in such a state is counter-productive (where our rational attempts to achieve a particular result end up by achieving its opposite), restrictive (where we simply cannot achieve a particular result by individual action), or socially contradictory (where we can only act as we wish at the expense of the possibility of another acting in the same way). Another way to put this is to say that we seek to avoid a "state of nature" situation when it leads to vicious cycles (the downward spiral into the tragedy of the commons), prevents virtuous cycles (the upward spiral in the provision of communal goods), or treats people as morally unequal (when rights come into conflict). In all such situations a good case can be made for the necessity of governance, and this implies that the range of our possible activities—our choices—must be limited in some way. But, we would suggest, *reasonable* people—those who have some concern for others—would not find such restrictions objectionable. They would not see them as infringements on their *Liberty* (even if, in some situations, they may find them annoying).

There is, however, a further element in this kind of liberal position which needs to be considered. While in some cases it is clear that a particular activity falls into one or other of these categories, this is not always the case. When we are considering things like murder, or which side of the road we drive on, it seems obvious enough, but in most other areas it is not. Indeed, there is virtually always some room for argument about such things, and at a multiplicity of different levels—this is the realm of politics.

Consider, for example, education. We would argue that this is clearly a communal good—in two different senses. Firstly, it is a communal good in that there is no point in one person having it unless other people do as well— for whom would they talk to? Secondly, and more importantly, it is a communal good because we gain from other people having it. That is, we all gain from living in an educated society, even if we are not particularly educated ourselves. As such, it is an activity in which there is clearly a role for government to play and, from our point of view, this should be an extensive role. But this might not be so obvious to others. They might, for instance, want to stress the individual economic benefits attached to education. Or, even if they accept its communal element, they might disagree with us about the extent of this benefit, and particularly about the amount of limited public resources which should be devoted to it. Even if we agreed thus far, there are still many possibilities for dispute about how such public resources should be utilised—and so on. The vital point here is that, from a liberal perspective, there is no authoritative way to *finalise* such a debate. While governments might need to make decisions about such matters when, for instance, they formulate their budgets, this is not taken as an end to the argument (indeed, it is usually the opposite). There is never a "last word" on such matters.

This is not the case in authoritarian systems. There the rulers can have the last word, for it is characteristic of such regimes that they do not take kindly to criticism. In liberal societies, in contrast, everything is at least potentially subject to criticism (even liberal theory itself). What counts is not *who* makes an argument, but the argument itself. This is the fundamental freedom which arises directly from the principle of moral equality. For if we are all, at some basic level, worthy of equal moral consideration, then the views which flow from our individual moral concerns are also equally worthy of consideration. This does not, of course, mean that all such views should be considered as equally *valid* (this is a common confusion). Some of the political views expressed in liberal societies will, no doubt, be illiberal, counter-productive, dangerous, or just plain silly, and they should be identified as such, but what cannot be countenanced is any attempt to prevent their expression. In liberal society such ideas are dealt with by argument (including argued dismissal), and not by repression.

More, in liberal societies it is not just that all political views (at the very least) should be allowed to be expressed, but that such expression should have the potential to be politically meaningful. That is, it is not just that people have the right to express their views on political matters, they have an equal right to organise in political groupings to attempt to have those ideas implemented. They have, in short, the right to be *political*. This is the area of fundamental freedom in liberal theory: political liberty. And it is clear that the kind of environmentalism we have outlined poses no threat to this kind of liberty. Indeed, the whole point of this work is to develop the kind of political *argument* which environmentalists might rely on to make their case. Moreover, through our examination of the "tragedy of the commons" and the "state of nature" our analysis not only provides a principled justification for government action, but one which is a logical development of those principles which have been fundamental to political liberalism since its origins.

This, we would accept, is probably a minority opinion—among both political theorists and active politicians. This is because the dominant strand of liberalism in western societies today is built primarily on the negative interpretation of Lockean views of the role of government rather than the positive strand we have emphasised. There are a number of reasons for this.

While it does make some sense to talk about a "Keynesian consensus" which was pre-eminent in policy-making in the 1950s and 1960s, this approach to political life has always had its detractors, and it is they who have now come to the fore. One of the most prominent of these was the Austrian economist Freidrick Hayek who, in books like *The Road to Serfdom*, pointed to what he saw as the dangers of "creeping socialism" arising from the increasingly regulatory and redistributive nature of western society. While there was a considerable irony in Hayek's title—for, as we have already pointed out, the institution of serfdom arose as a consequence of the breakdown of central government with the decline of the Roman Imperium—his argument meshed neatly with the general ideological tenor of the cold war period. And, as that war continued, similar kinds of views became increasingly prevalent.

At the same time, Keynesian economics, for all its manifest successes, was increasingly under attack at a theoretical level. More than any other period the 1950s and 1960s was a time when main-stream Social Science, particularly in the United States, attempted to truly earn the appellation of "science". In Sociology, Psychology, Political Science and, above all, Economics, an attempt was made to try and imitate the kind of "objective", "value-free" and mathematically precise qualities which were thought to be characteristic of the "hard sciences"—particularly Physics. This movement already had by far its strongest hold in what came to be known as "neo-classical economics". The starting point here, as we mentioned before, was the notion of a "perfectly free market", and this had two great advantages. The first was its apparent "value freedom"—for in considering a market one is seemingly only concerned with choices, based on a rational assessment of advantage, not with broader questions of value. The second is that, once this assumption is made, then it is possible to subject the actions of people in a market to mathematical analysis in a great deal of detail. The discipline of economics, then, could not only be presented as "hard-headed" and "scientific", and as clearly distinguishable from the "softer" and "fuzzier" areas of social inquiry, but could also be seen as a realm of genuine "expertise".

But Keynesianism did not fit neatly into this mould. Not only was it explicitly political—designed, as Keynes put it, to "save Capitalism from itself"—but its interventionist approach meant that the mathematical precision of free-market analysis could not always be applied. It was, from an academic point of view, simply "messy": concerned as much with judgement as with calculation. So, while Keynesian economics may have been taught, it was not particularly liked and, with some notable exceptions,[3] most prominent academic economists tended towards the neo-classical school, passing on this orientation to their students. When the "long boom" seemed to collapse in the early to mid 1970s[4] this reinforced the tendency to promote "neo-classical" over "Keynesian" approaches to economic management, and this rapidly carried over into the political arena. Again, there were a variety of historical factors which supported this tendency.

By the mid 1970s, and increasingly through the 1980s and 1990s, the politicians who began to emerge had a very different life experience to those who they began to replace. Rather than being children of depression and war, they had been shaped by the boom itself. And, while this period was no utopia, it was characterised by a high level of social and economic security. At the same time, it was also a period when government was increasingly looked at with some suspicion. This was not only because of the "cold-war" identification of "big" government with "authoritarian" government, it was also the public response to the war in Vietnam and the fact that, as only could be expected, some of the government bureaucracies had become insensitive, inefficient and ineffective. For those with no direct experience of the horrors of the Depression or the effectiveness of government activity during the war and the early period of post-war reconstruction, it was easy to perceive government regulation as simply intrusive, forgetting its fundamental rationale.

At the same time, political parties of all ideological persuasions had become more professional—in two different ways. At an organisational level they had developed their levels of expertise, typically beginning to hire professional political and economic analysts, rather than relying so heavily on the "amateurs" who had risen through the party ranks for advice and policy formulation. And the politicians themselves now tended to be more "professional"—typically more highly educated (frequently in Law) and more affluent. This changed the character of the parties. Both the old style conservatism of parties of the right, and the democratic socialism of the left, began to give way to an apparent "middle-ground", which was critical of government itself and increasingly economically "dry". It also changed the character of elections. These were now less seen, at least within the parties themselves, as ideological struggles, and more and more as simply contests to be won or lost. But behind these contests there was a considerable consensus—a mixture of neo-classical economics and neo-classical liberalism—and the catch-cries became much the same: "privatisation", "deregulation" and "reductions in government expenditure".

And the key point about this particular amalgam of political and economic views is that, while at one level it is deeply—if implicitly—ideological, at another it is profoundly anti-political. Where Keynesianism had quite explicitly attempted to subvert the economics of the "free" market to meet political purposes, this approach subverts political purposes to economic aims—to the demands of the "market". Increasingly it is economic indicators—of a particular kind—which are taken to be the proper measure of the success or failure of governments. And, typically, these are the measures which suit only one section of society. So, for example, in Australia the present federal treasurer, Mr Peter Costello, is happy to claim that the government "has got the economic fundamentals right", without any reference to the high rates of unemployment and growing inequality which have characterised the last twenty five years. In this kind of mentality the profitability of the business (and particularly the financial) sector is all. It is simply assumed that this kind of "healthy" economy translates into a better life for everyone (or at least the majority), even when there is evidence to the contrary.

What environmentalism requires is a reassertion of the political over the economic. For what our analysis has shown is that it is precisely the logic of the "free" market which leads to the kind of vicious cycles which spiral down into tragedies of the commons, and prevents the development of the potentially virtuous cycles which might build and enhance a variety of communal and environmental goods. While this may involve some restrictions on our economic freedoms (to, for example, use resources as wastefully as we want, or to pollute where we wish), it involves no threat to our political freedoms. Indeed, it does quite the opposite—for it involves a reassertion of the political demand that governments should act in the interests of their citizenry—for the benefit of all the people, not just for that essentially metaphysical entity called the Economy. And it is in the environmental arena where the nature of those interests can be seen most clearly—in both the potentials for disaster and the possibilities for improvement. What this involves is not some new form of politics, but a resurgence *of* politics.

The first element of such a resurgence requires the development (or re-development) of what we refer to as "institutional intelligence" in government. While we will have more to say about this in the next chapter, there are two points which need to be made at this stage. The first concerns the nature of elections, and the second the broader structure of governance.

Elections can be seen as the central means to institutional intelligence in liberal democratic polities—in the sense that they are mechanisms whose purpose is to keep the government's "mind on the job". This, after all, is what they were designed to do. When James Mill convinced Jeremy Bentham that the franchise should be extended to all citizens, not just to land holders, and had this policy incorporated into liberal programs, it was precisely on this basis. He argued that it was only when all groups in society were represented that you could expect governments to act in the interests of all—rather than just a single class of people. The first thing to note about this formulation is that it is not—except in the most general sense—about transmitting the "will" (understood in terms of "opinions") of the people from voter to representative. While many governments like to claim that their election has given them a "mandate" to carry out some policy as an expression of the "will of the people", elections are really far too crude an instrument to perform this function. It is never really clear why an electorate votes in the way it does. There is always more than one issue to be considered in an election, and how a population of voters balances out a range of differing concerns is never transparent to even quite sophisticated forms of analysis. All elections can really tell us is whether a majority (or at least a significant proportion—depending upon the electoral system) of voters feel that the government of the day has done a "good job" or whether is should be replaced. It is, in short, the role of governments to govern, and the role of the electorate to judge how well they have performed that task.

It is this role of electoral systems which had been muddied by the professionalisation of the parties, and the rise of "opinion poll" styles of politics which accompanied this. To the extent that the focus of many political parties has moved from providing good government as they see it—and allowing the electorate to judge on this—to winning the next election at any cost—by attempting to be all things to all people—then elections have lost some of their effectiveness as instruments of institutional intelligence. This has encouraged the tendency for Governments, made up of politicians who are anti-political, to create policy regimes which are explicitly anti-government. Environmentalism, as we have described it, has much to offer here. For, in its focus on the commons—on the background of social existence—it has a clear theory of government, of its purpose and aims, and of what needs to be achieved for the common good. It has, in short, a sense of the positive role of government, and it is this which seems to be lacking in so many of the major political groupings. As such, it has the potential to counter the kind of political malaise which is apparent in so many of the liberal democracies.

The other area where environmentalism has a great deal to contribute is at an organisational level. For, while "Green" Governments may have to be larger—in the sense that they would be involved in a wider range of activities—there is no requirement that they should be monolithic. Indeed, precisely because they are concerned with the politics of the "commons" their natural tendency is in the opposite direction. Commons—whether environmental, economic, social or cultural—are, as we have shown, pervasive in our lives, but they are also diverse. Many commons are highly local in nature, the concerns of particular communities or sections of communities, others are so pervasive as to be essentially global in character, while most lie somewhere between these extremes. And the most effective organisational means to manage such commons would also reflect this diversity. The role of government is not so much to manage directly all commons as to set general guidelines for management, and to facilitate the creation of organisational regimes appropriate to particular commons. Some commons need to be managed locally, others regionally or nationally, and some will require the development of international organisations. In many cases the "seeds" of such organisations already exist, and it would be the aim of a "green" government to help them develop and grow. The aim, in short, should be towards the creation of a strong and vigorous "civil society".

This is not a new proposal. Many in what is called the "communitarian" school of social and political thought also see this aim as highly desirable. But, unlike most communitarians, who wish to simply moralise such communities into existence, the kind of environmentalism we have outlined recognises that the development of a healthy civil society requires more than moral exhortation. It recognises, in the first instance, that the kind of organisations which go to make up a strong civil society are typically built around a commons of one kind or another. While in some cases this may be the "moral" commons of, say, a church group, it is far more frequent for them to be built around one of the environmental, economic or social commons we have already mentioned. And the point about such commons, and the organisations concerned with them, is that people are willing to participate in their management because they gain something from it. There is no accident to the fact that "commons" and "community" derive from the same linguistic root.

It also recognises that, while in some sense all such groups must be built from the "ground up"—that there is a "grass-roots" element to their existence—that Government, nevertheless, has an important role to play in this area. And this role is not just to aid with the provision of the kind of expertise or the regulatory regime which might be required, but also through the provision of real resources. A dynamic and healthy civil society of the kind we have envisaged can only be built, at least in our type of society, when Governments are willing to put time, energy and, most of all, money into its creation. Again, the general point is clear. The solutions to the kinds of problems which face us, in the social as much as the environmental sphere, can only come out of a genuinely political process. And this cannot be a politics which is simply subservient to the economic realm. For where economics (at least in theory) is concerned with efficiency, politics is, at its very core, concerned with equity.

Notes

1   Eg, Francis Fukuyama, *The End of History and the Last Man*, (London: Hamish Hamilton, 1992).

2   T. H. Green, *Lectures on the Principles of Political Obligation*, (Cambridge: Cambridge University Press, 1986).

3   Probably the most prominent being John Kenneth Galbraith.

4   The reasons for this collapse are complex and controversial, but a case can be made that it was not the product of some inherent failure in Keynesianism. See, for example Tim Battin, *Abandoning Keynes: Australia's Capital Mistake*, (London: Macmillan, 1997).

8 Recovering Politics

By this stage in our argument we have outlined the basic features of political ecology, and so of the task of the political ecologist. For while our account of political ecology has been developed against the background of environmental threats, their analysis in terms of the logic of the tragedy of the commons points to the role and place of politics more generally. Politics should be seen as the guardian of those background conditions which, protected from the ravages of foreground decision-making in the state of nature, provide the arena for the kind of organised and sustainable life in which individual freedom becomes a boon and not a threat to all. This move from a purely environmental focus to the broader ecology of the background does not involve an abandonment or weakening of our environmental concerns. It is, rather, a way of deepening those concerns by integrating them with issues of material security and social justice—an integration forced on us as soon as we abandon Locke's mistaken, if historically understandable, faith in environmental plenitude over scarcity. It would be a sad thing indeed if the misguided pursuit of environmental "purity" prevented us from uncovering and developing the ecological promise of that politics which lies at the heart of the modern world.

In our formulation environmental concern leads to an inclusive political ecology, with political ecology defined as the politics of those background conditions essential to a successful and sustainable social life. And it is a certain kind of politics of the background, one we are willing to call Lockean, though undoubtedly this is a label much abused in the history of political thought, and for reasons we discussed in the previous chapter. Now is the moment to say more about this Lockean understanding of political ecology, both to make the nomenclature more acceptable, and to uncover further the logic of successful institutional solutions to the tragedy of the commons.

To begin let us recall the three strategies Hardin recommends as solutions to these problems: moralism, privatisation, and authoritarianism. Each fails for its own reasons, but beneath these failures there lies a common fault. Moralism fails because it inevitably sees the notion of goodness and virtue, as they apply to the individual who refrains from strategies destructive of the background conditions of social life, move ever closer to the notions of naivety and self-damaging stupidity. Privatisation alone can be guaranteed to fail because rather than suppressing or metamorphosing those attitudes and motives which generate the tragedy of the commons, it simply entrenches them further and more intractably into the world. Authoritarianism fails to the degree that it makes power the prisoner of arbitrary, so unreliable, decision-making. In each case the real failure turns out to be the same—the failure to construct intelligent institutional arrangements which reliably and sustainably offer people the possibility, the *attractive* possibility, of "doing the right thing". But what *are* the ingredients for these intelligent institutions, and for the institutional intelligence of those able, sensibly now, without stupidity or a groundless faith in arbitrary power, to pursue individually and mutually beneficial strategies of living?

In previous chapters we worked our way towards an answer by dealing first with those economistic biases which incline many to reject politics for unrestricted privatisation, and second by pointing to the dangers and misconceptions involved in offering instead a politics of authoritarianism. We suggested instead a politics not primarily of coercion but of "common agreement to general restraint", and identified this with the style of answer Locke proposed in opposition to Hobbes. However it can easily seem that by itself the mere idea of a "social contract" is too abstract, too disconnected from the realities of "really existing" governance, to take us much beyond the merely platitudinous, *viz.*, that it is the creation of rational agreement between the relevant parties. This vacuity has not, unfortunately, prevented much paper and ink (if not always too much thought) being expended on endless articles, tracts and books which in effect simply repeat the truism, though typically dressed in Habermasian clothes so that "discourse" is somehow of itself felt able to create the conditions of its inevitable success in the face of all and any problems whatsoever, including everything environmental.

It is our view that we have had enough talk about talk in these areas. The incantationary insistence of the need for "discursive politics" or "discursive democracy" may have its place at a primitive stage of reflection on the Lockean conception of political ecology, but it is at most a gesture, not a destination, and at worse it is positively pernicious as "consultation" becomes a means for obscuring the real operations of authority.[1]

It is here that we are fortunate to have Elinor Ostrom's seminal work on the evolution of institutions for collective action in *Governing the Commons*. For while Ostrom's study of various social commons regimes does not make the general connection between commons and governance which defines political ecology, her theoretical and empirical work can be placed in this framework, and in a way that lets us avoid the suspicion of offering comforting truisms rather than instructive analysis.

Ostrom considers a number of "long-enduring, self-organised, and self-governed" social commons regimes (she calls them *Common Property Regimes*): from thousand year old Swiss mountain commons, Spanish and Philippine irrigation commons, Turkish and Sri Lankan fishing commons, to recently established commons regimes for Californian artesian basin management; and in each case uncovers the critical importance of a set of "design principles" in ensuring the viability and long-term effectiveness of these institutional arrangements. Let us approach these "principles", and their importance for the political ecologist, through a brief account of one of the successful social commons regimes she discusses.

In semi-arid Southern Spain in 1435, 84 irrigators dependent on two canals from the Turia River gathered at a monastery determined to sort out the problems caused by competitive and unrestricted access to a valuable, variable, and deeply finite water resource. They agreed on a regulatory system, an institutional regime, which specified who had water rights, how that water was to be shared, how canal maintenance responsibilities were to be shared, what officials were to be elected and how, and how penalties were to be attached to violations of the agreement. The agreement, flexibly developed, still operates, and operates effectively over 550 years later. Here then is a stable solution to the problem of sustainability in the face of a threatened tragedy of the commons. So let us look at the system they constructed and how it operates.

To begin with, water-rights inhere in the land adjacent to the canals, and permit access to an amount of the total available supplies of water proportional to the size of the relevant holdings. Water is distributed in turn (*por tourno*) from the head to the tail of each canal (*heurta*). The order in which the irrigators can receive water is fixed, though each irrigator, outside the special conditions drought imposes, decides how long to keep the headgate open, subject only to the condition that they use the water on their land, and that they do not waste it. If irrigators miss their turn, then they must wait until the next round of ordered distribution.

It follows from the nature of the distributional scheme that adjacent irrigators are well-placed and well-motivated to engage in low cost monitoring of the activities of their fellows so as to ensure they keep to the rules, though of course as the logic of the tragedy of the commons implies, this will only be effective to the extent that there exists a legitimate and authoritative organisational structure successfully defining and defending those rules. Thus each *heurta* meets together every few years and elects from their number a syndic who can be seen as a kind of Chief Executive Officer for the community, charged with upholding and implementing the traditional rules and practices of successful management of the *heurta,* including dealing with disputes. The syndic typically has allocated a small staff of ditch-riders and guards to help them carry out their duties. The syndic is bound to consult with, and defer to the decisions of, an elected executive committee (*junta de gobierno*) composed of delegates from all the main service areas of the *heurta,* particularly where matters of canal maintenance are involved.

Because the canals are part of a connected hydrological system, each *heurta's* syndic participates with his fellows syndics in two weekly tribunals, one essentially judicial, the other a body for political deliberation. The first is a water court (*Tribunal de las Aguas*), where disputes concerning rule-violations, and appeals against a syndic's decisions on such matters, are heard. The court has a presiding officer who has an inquisitorial role, though decisions are determined by the entire court, excluding the syndic of the *heurta* from which the dispute or appeal originates. The court's decision in such cases is determined by its understanding of that *heurtas* particular rules, though it is noticeable both how few disputes actually come to it, and how small typically are the penalties attached to infractions of the rules. The second tribunal assumes more the role of a management and co-ordinating body for all the associated *heurta*. It concerns itself mainly with problems of intercanal coordination, and centrally those to do with determining then instituting the operational procedures of the irrigation season, given the amount of water available at the time. Given the variability of flow in the Turia this is particularly important, and especially when drought occurs as it does commonly enough. In such extreme circumstances the syndics, as representatives of their own *heurta*, and answerable to its executive committee, are responsible for determining how long each irrigator has water, a period determined both on the basis of the personal needs of each irrigator, and on the collective impact of such need provision on the possibilities of meeting the needs of others.

When Ostrom analyses the striking success of the *heurta* system she finds eight crucial "design principles": principles she finds too in her analysis of all those other successful social commons regimes she investigates. Let us begin our discussion of her findings by simply listing her principles, then discussing them in the light of the Lockean logic of political ecology. That logic enables us to see why these empirically located common principles *are* indeed common—what it is that makes them, and uniformly across successful social commons regimes, a "package-deal"—at the same time as deepening and refining her analysis. But before that let us make a very important point, particularly in the context of contemporary discussion of environmentalism and politics. For what we have in the *heurta* system is, as Ostrom says, a "long-enduring" social commons regime. The water resources of the Turia have been effectively managed for irrigation purposes for over half a millennium, perhaps even a millennium. Not only is this an extraordinary feat of flexible endurance spanning significant climate change and large-scale political, social and economic disruption, it enables us to give a *non-metaphorical, a strict and literal,* account of "environmental sustainability". Rather than an idle phrase we have an example, an instance, of environmental and institutional sustainability: an example indeed which shows how the one depends upon the other so closely as to be either side of the same coin.

What then is the currency of success for the *heurta* system? It involves Ostrom argues i) "clearly defined boundaries, where this means a clear set of property-rights which distinguish the 'insider' from the 'outsider', and which delineate the boundaries of the resource to be managed"; ii) it generates and sustains "congruence between appropriation and provision rules and local conditions"; iii) it rests on "collective choice arrangements" so that those on the "inside" can participate in modifying and altering rules when necessary; iv) it establishes a system of monitoring, so that insiders are both well-informed as to the operations of the institution, and are held accountable for their resource management decisions; v) it involves a system of "graduated sanctions" by which insiders are penalised for management breaches so that their fellows are reassured in their commitment to proper adherence, while at the same time the penalties are not so extreme as to alienate, rather than reintegrate violators; and vi) it provides "conflict-resolution measures" which are recognised as legitimate because representative and impartial, which effectively decide disputes between insiders. To these six design principles, all easily located in our sketch of the *heurta* system, Ostrom adds two more: vii) that insiders (or potential insiders) must have a general, and politically recognised, right to organise their own social commons regime; and viii) that such social commons regimes permit a "nested" structure so that smaller organisations can fit into larger, more inclusive systems without undermining their essential "autonomy".

It is not difficult to locate these conditions in the example of the *heurta* system, and we do not wish to labour the point, but there are a number of lessons to be drawn from Ostrom's account. To begin with the "principles" fit naturally into the Lockean account of the move from the state of nature to political life. Thus an impending tragedy of the commons is met by the formation of a community out of that concern. As we might put it: the community arises from a private concern for well-being, refracted through a recognition that here individuals are all "in the same life-boat", so that "going it alone" offers not hope but disaster. This is a concern and a refraction environmentalism establishes on the very deepest levels of life and survival. What emerges when the commons is closed is a *social* commons centred on protection and preservation of the necessary background conditions for worthwhile individual lives. Here lies the basis of that democratic and communitarian element which demands collective choice arrangements and sensitive and sensible systems of monitoring and conflict-resolution. More particularly, we see in the emergence of a social commons a political and organisational structure that is essentially "bottom-up", not "top-down" as in the Hobbesian model. Power originates from the social commons, that is to say, it begins from mutually recognised insiders (or "stakeholders") as they form a community, and then (if necessary) flows upwards, through voting, representation and accountability, while authoritative decisions for the regime flow downwards, subject always to rights of appeal and the possibility of "opting out" of the system. As part of this bottom-up dynamic, the local knowledge of insiders is effectively utilised and so is able continually to inform decision-making and so sustain commitment in a way Hobbesian systems cannot. It follows from this that Ostrom's second design principle— "congruence between appropriation and provision rules and local conditions"—is not so much a design principle as simply the mark of the successful utilisation of the "social contract" as a solution to the problems of the open commons.

There is one essential constituent of a social commons regime Ostrom's account leaves merely implicit, but which it is vital to make explicit, for in a very real sense it is the tectonic plate on which the whole regime depends and moves. In our account of the *heurta* system we saw that the *needs* of the irrigators, individually and collectively, were vital in determining the allocation and provision of resources; this is especially so in times of drought, but also in times of plenty as the individual irrigator decides how long his head-gate remains open to the flow. This needs-based focus is no accident in such sustainable regimes, though it is a truth we are in danger of forgetting in today's political climate. After all, the *social* commons itself arises because everyone's needs are threatened by the short-term pursuit of individual advantage. Here is the essential *insurance* role played by social commons regimes; a role which is crucial to sustaining the social contract. For no-one can be expected to continue to participate willingly in such a regime if it systematically or otherwise ignores the very conditions of viable existence through failures to internalise risk. Notice too that this essential welfarist element does not threaten the "Soviet" result under which effort and ability are derided as themselves stupid. In the *heurta* system the irrigator who uses water most efficiently and effectively is rewarded for his or her efforts, and the commitment to "needs-insurance" respects this. Thus an irrigator who might have planted a higher cost but more water hungry crop has in times of plenty the ability to increase the amount of water utilised, while in times of scarcity this additional investment is taken into account in assigning the period for flow reception.

If, once the importance of equity is revealed, Ostrom's account has anything special to add to the Lockean account of politics, it lies with the last two conditions she points to. For Locke's account, for those historical reasons already discussed, has an insistent focus on the background politics of security and justice in the framework of the nation-state which encourages many to miss the applicability of his account to problems of governance on other scales, both larger and smaller. This fault is not, however, intrinsic to the Lockean approach. On the contrary, the idea of "nested enterprises" gives an explicit formulation to the idea of "civil society" so important to Locke, and helps clarify the role of the state as the protector of this realm.

You will recall that the logic of the tragedy of the commons threatens whenever individual agents' rational pursuit of self-interest tend to undermine the background conditions of such agency itself; and, of course, such agents can be groups rather than lone individuals. To solve such problems we apply the Lockean logic on a new level, just as in the *heurta* system autonomous canal organisations come together to constitute more inclusive levels of organisation, driven from below, rather than imposed unilaterally from above. The state is simply the most inclusive social commons regime around. It has no special, and no unique powers. Sovereignty is often pointed to here as the mark of such uniqueness and interpreted in authoritarian terms, but in the Lockean framework, not the Hobbesian, this is a mistaken identification. Sovereignty means rather, first, that the state should function as a "final court of *appeal*", and second, that it defends and furthers the formation of those social commons regimes necessary to deal with our emerging environmental problems. These two and connected tasks do not give the state a unique existence for they are inherent in all social commons regimes, but in context they do give it a definite task, and one of vital importance. At the very least it will be called upon to do much more than the "minimal state" defended by those on the Right who see government action as always bearing the tincture of authoritarianism.

In particular the state, like all other social commons regimes, cannot, for the political ecologist, ignore questions of *needs* — issues of *equity*. For it is clear that the sustainability of the kind of organisations we have discussed is directly dependent on their ability to meet the needs of those involved in them. If these needs are not met, or even are perceived as not being met, then it becomes entirely rational (indeed, for Locke, it is an imperative) to opt out of the system—to revert to a state of nature, even with all the tragedy this entails. And this is not only the case in the environmental arena, but in the political and economic arena more generally. It is here, in its forceful reminder of the importance of *needs*, that political ecology has so much to offer the more "mainstream" styles of political thought. However, before we can develop this point further, we should digress (if only briefly) to consider the nature of "needs" and how, if at all, they can be distinguished from "wants".

This is an important task, for in the dominant economic world-view this distinction has little or no place. Indeed, many economists forcefully deny, and teach this denial to their students, that such a distinction can be made. As an academic economist friend of ours is fond of remarking "a need is just something you want, which you don't want to pay for". But, while this conflation of "needs" and "wants" may be particularly useful to the economic theorist—removing, as it does, any ethical dimension from those preferences which can now be given a simple dollar value—it obscures much which is vital to a full understanding of the implications of a developed political ecology.

For all the denial of our economist friend, "needs" are different things from "wants", and not just because we have two different words to describe them. Furthermore, this distinction is not just a matter of emphasis—so that "needs" are merely stronger, or more urgent, versions of "wants"—there is a fundamental difference—it is indeed, in a different guise, the difference between background and foreground—which is central to our political, as well as our economic, activity. The key point here is that while our "needs" may also be our "wants"—so that we "need" food, if we are to survive, and when we are hungry we also "want" it—this is not always the case. We can have "wants" that could hardly be considered "needs", "needs" which are not "wants", and even "needs" which we do not know about. So, for example, it could be the case that one of us is an undiagnosed diabetic. If this were the case, it would make perfect sense to say that we "need" insulin even though, being unaware of our condition, we do not "want" it. Further, even if we became aware of our "need", it may well be the case that, because of a particular abhorrence to needles, we still do not "want" it in any genuine sense. The other side of the case is even easier to make. For while we may "need" food and drink, it would be very odd (except in a rhetorical or satirical sense) for us to suggest that we "needed" caviar or champagne, though we may very well "want" them.

"Wants" refer to our desires, but our "needs" are those things which, if we do not have them, will harm us in some significant way.[2] Another way of putting this is to point out that if we do not achieve our "wants" then we may well be disappointed, but if we do not gain our "needs" then our lives will be blighted. We may "want" caviar and champagne and, because of our economic circumstances, have to make do with lesser fare, but this is a very different situation to the fate of a severely malnourished child whose physical and mental abilities could be permanently damaged because of their lack of adequate nourishment.

There are two general points which should be made before we return to our broader discussion. The first is that "needs" can be socially and culturally specific. So, for example, it makes real sense to say that our medieval herdsman did not "need" the skills of literacy and numeracy in the same way as does a resident of a modern industrial society. The second is that while some "needs" may be essentially individual, the ones we are primarily concerned with in political life are those which are universal—so that all humans need food— or which are general within particular groups and communities: the herdsman may not need to be literate, but all herdsmen need the skills of animal husbandry, which may well be irrelevant to the city dweller.

All of this has real import. For where in the post-war era, with the memories of depression and war fresh in their minds, people, and the politicians who represented them, focused public policy on the provision of needs, ushering in a era where levels of overall equality and equity were gradually improved, this is no longer the case. The language of "need" has increasingly been replaced by the language of "want", typically expressed through notions of "free choice". And this has been the ultimate justification for all those familiar policy prescriptions which dominate the ideological landscape of most western societies. So, while at one level the calls for the privatisation of public enterprises, the introduction of user-pays systems in a range of public services, and reductions in public spending more generally, have been justified in terms of "efficiency", what underlies this notion is the idea of "want satisfaction".

Theoretically (if not always in practice), the more "efficient" an economic system is, the better the match between the allocation of resources and the satisfaction of preferences—of wants. And, the more "wants" that are satisfied the "better" or "stronger" the economy. This, after all, is what GDP per capita, at least putatively, measures. But, and as was implicit in our earlier discussion of these issues, all of this depends on there being no distinction made between "needs" and "wants": $10,000 dollars spent on gold-plated taps for a millionaire's mansion counts exactly the same as $10,000 spent on providing food and shelter for the homeless.

From an ecological perspective, "needs" must have priority over "wants", even if this means that "preferences" are not satisfied as "efficiently" as might otherwise be the case. Indeed (and again) this is what the logic of the tragedy of the commons shows us. For another way of reading this tragedy is as the result of the triumph of immediate wants over the sustainable provision of needs. As the herdsman follow their immediate foreground preference—to increase their herds, and thereby their profits—the result is to destroy the commons itself, and thereby to undermine that background necessary for the possibility of satisfying not merely future wants, but those very survival needs essential to such a future. The point is that, typically, the kinds of environmental goods we seek are *needs*, and universal needs at that. It is not just, for instance, that we have a preference for clean air or water, or healthy food, but that, if we do not get these things, we will all be irrecoverably harmed. At the level of individual preference some of us may well be willing to trade-off immediate want satisfaction against such long term needs—hence the tragedy of the commons—but to allow this at the level of communal (or *political*) decision-making would clearly be irrational, for all (or, at the very least, a majority) must ultimately lose.

So, a primary focus on needs is central to a genuinely Green politics. And it is not just that those environmental goods we seek to enhance are vital to people's real needs; it is also, as our earlier analysis shows, an organisational imperative if we are to build the kind of institutional arrangements which can effectively and sustainably manage and maintain these goods. And this means that a concern with equity—with social justice and equality—is *central* to Green politics.

Many on the Green side of politics have glimpsed this truth—as in the Australian Greens' Senator Bob Brown's call for "Environmental protection *and* social justice *and* grass-roots democracy"—but the real point is that these should not be regarded as simply a list of (however compatible) aims. Rather, it should be recognised that they are the *one* aim. Environmental protection *is* social justice *is* grass-roots democracy.

This follows directly from our consideration of Ostrom's resource management regimes. The kind of sustainable and effective institutional arrangements she describes are built from the bottom-up, but can be "nested" into a range of higher level organisations—all the way up to the level of the nation-state, and in some cases even further. This is simply a model of the kind of grass-roots democracy which those theorists who have stressed the importance of a strong and vigorous "civil society" for democratic life more generally have always looked to. But the connection with issues of social justice and equity is, it often seems, somewhat less obvious to many of us. A point largely attributable to a kind of ideological blindness which surrounds the most common instrument associated with issues of equity in our kind of society—the "welfare system".

When most people think of the welfare system they tend to associate it with a particular type of transfer payments. When we think of "welfare" we think of unemployment or sickness benefits or, sometimes, old age pensions. So, welfare is about transferring money from the moderately wealthy, *via* the medium of taxation, to the poor, allowing them to meet at least some of their needs. However, while these kinds of payments may be necessary in a civilised society—for if we do not make them then we are effectively forcing particular groups of people into crime or beggary or needless suffering—they are only the tip of the iceberg in the provision of welfare, and they can do little in themselves to improve significantly the degree of equity in society.

The first point to be made is that there is a great deal of hypocrisy in this area. It is not uncommon, for example, for those who rail against the recipients of unemployment or single parent benefits, to be quite sanguine about the subsidies they receive for the private schooling of their children or their private health insurance, or the "breaks" which allow them to minimise their taxation. In fact, every payment, subsidy, free service or means of legal tax avoidance made available by government can be perceived as a kind of transfer payment—the provision of welfare. This, after all, is how government is ultimately justified; as a means to improve our well-being, our welfare. It is just that, too often, and particularly for those who are both wealthy and self righteous, the benefits the poor receive are "undeserved", while the (often quite substantial) benefits that they receive are seen simply as their "due".

Basically this is just another example of foreground versus background thinking. The monetary benefits the poor receive are highly visible, while those received by middle and high income earners have simply blended into the inertial background. More importantly, this kind of foreground thinking obscures much of the real basis of equity (or inequity) in society. For, while direct monetary payments to the impoverished are, undoubtedly, a necessary means to improve equity in our kind of society, much more can be achieved in this area through the provision of common rather than individual goods. And, as we have already stressed in earlier chapters, environmental goods are, typically, common goods—by their very nature. If we improve the quality of the air in a city then this must benefit all who live there. Equity is built into such improvements: for my need for clean air to be satisfied I must also satisfy yours.

It could even be argued that making these kinds of improvements to the common goods available is the best possible means of improving the levels of genuine equity in society. While much more could be done in the foreground, in the collection of taxation and the provision of benefits, it is in the background that the real gains can be made. So, for example, even if I have little in the way of monetary resources, my life would be improved—my needs and wants more fully met—if I can breath clean air, drink potable water, be confident that the food I consume is unadulterated, swim in a pristine river, lake or ocean, walk in a park or wilderness area, fish in an unpolluted stream, read from the local library, and so on. And it is in the nature of such goods that they are communal in character: if they are to be effectively provided they must be provided to all who are effected by them.

While it is true that the very wealthy may be able to avoid some of the more obvious negative effects of our increasing environmental problems by, for example, living in leafy suburbs, well away from polluting factories and traffic, or by removing themselves entirely from the worst effected areas, increasingly this is no longer a viable option or, if it is, one which itself involves a significant diminution of choice. The reason people now talk of an "environmental crisis" is largely because the effects of environmental degradation are increasingly difficult to localise, and the solutions are even more so. It is impossible to solve the problems of air pollution in Hollywood unless we do so in the Los Angeles basin more generally, or the problems of Sydney Harbour's pollution in Mosman without dealing with the Parramatta river and Sydney Cove. This is even more obvious when we consider global environmental issues. We are all going to be (indeed in all probability already are being) affected by global warming, the decrease in the ozone layer and, ultimately, by declining levels of bio-diversity. Again, if we are to solve these problems we must do so for everyone.

Green politics, then, is not accidentally, but inherently a politics of equity. Its stress on the significance of environmental goods—which are, at the same time, background goods, communal goods, commons, and needs—naturally draws our attention to other areas of human existence where the same broad logic applies. In fact, because no clear distinction can be made between environmental goods and the kinds of economic, social, and cultural goods we described earlier, any effective solution to environmental problems will and must have a significant impact on these other areas of our lives.

Consider, again, the example of air pollution in our major cities. While there may be various sources of this pollution it is clear that emissions from motor vehicles contribute a significant amount. There may be various technical "fixes" which can help to reduce this problem, but the more effective way would be by trying to significantly reduce the use of motor vehicles, and this can best be done through much greater use of public transport. But, how could such a significant increase in usage be achieved? Apart from draconian regulation of vehicle use—which would not only be politically unpopular but probably ineffective[3]—the most obvious way would be by encouraging people to want to use the public system to meet their need for transport. This would require the development of a system of transport which fulfilled a number of requirements.

Firstly, such a system would have to be effective: it would have to allow people to get from one location to another in a reasonable period of time, in a reasonable degree of comfort, and in safety (at least the equivalent of what they could achieve in their own vehicles). Secondly, it would have to be reliable and regular, so that people could be confident that they could reach their destinations, even if they had not memorised the relevant timetables. And thirdly, and perhaps most importantly, it would have to be inexpensive— obviously less than the marginal cost of driving one's own vehicle. But while such systems are, fairly obviously technically feasible, and would significantly reduce pollution, their development will not take place without a high level of political support.

The problem is that while such systems may be effective in achieving the aim of reductions in vehicle use, and technically efficient in terms of energy and resource usage, they are unlikely to be economically efficient, when this is understood in its narrowest sense. Almost certainly such a system would never be developed on a purely free-market basis (although it could have a significant private component), and might well require significant government support to remain in operation. This is basically because the free market's emphasis is essentially on profits, and the other aims of the system would always be over-ridden if these were threatened. Yet, from a broader economic perspective it could be highly economically efficient. Even if such a system required government subsidy, and this had to be funded by increased taxation, the savings to the community more generally, in the reduction of all those negative externalities associated high levels of motor vehicle use, as well as the positive environmental and other benefits of such a system, would almost certainly outweigh the cost of the subsidies involved.

There is another thing to note about such a system. It is not just that it would provide economic and environmental benefits to the community at large, but it would do so in a way which was essentially equitable. Although all benefit in a general sense, the existence of reliable, and *cheap*, transport constitutes an obvious boon to those on lower incomes, who might have little alternative in a less effective system. Their *need* for transport (for, say, employment purposes) can now be met, at the same time as the needs of all, for both transport and a better environment, are satisfied. This would not get rid of all inequalities (and this is hardly the aim in any case)—the rich could still have Rolls Royces in their garages—but it would increase equity in such communities, as the needs of the whole population are met more effectively.

And, if this is the underlying logic of Green politics, then it also applies in a range of areas which are not so obviously "environmental" in character. So, for example, it makes explicable the Australian Greens' opposition to the privatisation of Telstra—Australia's largest, and largely publicly owned, telecommunications company. Here the grounds are not so directly "environmental" (although, clearly, a public company can be held more accountable in this area) as equitable: the real fear that an industry in this area run on pure market lines would take little account of the need, particularly of those in remote and rural areas, for reasonable access to the telecommunication system. It would, in effect, involve the destruction of a commons for little more than short-term political gain.

Of course, it will not always be the case that issues concerning the environment and a concern with equity (except in its long-term and most general sense) will fall so neatly into line as in the example of public transport in large cities. There is little doubt, if we are to take environmental protection seriously, that there will be many instances where particular individuals and groups will find themselves worse off. So, for example, if we are to reduce the rate of the reckless exploitation of resources—in areas as diverse as forestry, fishing, mining and irrigation—then this will mean that employment is reduced in these industries. In such cases it can be argued that we are providing a good to the community at the expense of those who now find themselves out of work, or who might have been employed if we allowed such industries to expand. Indeed, it is this kind of argument which is always used by those who wish to increase their exploitation of resources, regardless of the environmental effects.

However, this kind of argument simply misses the point. For those inclined to make this kind of argument often champion "economic efficiency" in other areas, regardless of the employment consequences. A reduction of employment in forestry, in order to protect wilderness areas, is somehow seen as a great crime, while a reduction of employment in, say, banking—in order to increase corporate profits—is simply rational economic activity. More importantly, and as we pointed out in an earlier chapter, a Green approach to economic management does not merely consist in preventing things from happening, it requires a great deal of investment and activity in a whole range of areas. To move toward a genuinely sustainable and non-polluting form of energy usage, to give just one example, will require a very significant economic effort and generate an equally significant amount of employment. When we add all the other areas where large scale changes would be required then there is little doubt that a genuine Green approach to economic management can generate much more employment than it would destroy—even to the extent of achieving the kind of employment rates which were the normal expectation in the 1950s and 1960s. And, again, to achieve such employment rates will itself do a great deal to improve the general levels of equity in our kind of society.

In fact it is clearly the case that it has been the process of privatisation and corporatisation of public utilities which has led to significant reductions in employment, and this is no accident. The whole point of privatisation and corporatisation is to change the focus of an organisation from the provision of needs to the creation of profit, and one of the key elements in the profitability of any organisation is the size of the wage bill. Reduce this and profits can be increased, even if this means that, in the long term, the needs of many can no longer be adequately met. To re-focus significant areas of economic activity toward the provision of needs rather than profits is not to threaten employment but to create it and, in doing so, to help to reverse the trend to growing inequality which has characterised western society for the past two and a half decades.

Issues of equity, then, appear at every level of the Green political program. This arises directly out of the initial concern for human welfare, which must focus on the meeting of needs. It is a vital component of the organisational imperative to build sustainable institutions to preserve and enhance our common resources. And it is the necessary product of the kind of policies

Green politics implies. Even more, Political Ecology, as we have described it, is essentially a politics of commons and, thereby, of community. If we wish to build the kind of sense of community which will be required to solve our environmental problems then we must start to look at people in a different way: not as the desperate preference maximisers in the competition of all against all which is the "free" market, but as potentially cooperative seekers for common goods bound together in a social contract to avoid the kind of tragic environmental, economic and social disasters which now face us all. With this aim at its centre Political Ecology promises a reinvigoration of the kind of political vision at the heart of liberal democratic society.

Notes

1   In the normal run of things 'stake-holder' and 'community consultation' actually comes last, the final mystificatory step in the **DAD** progression so favoured by governments and business, *viz.,* **D**ecide, **A**nnounce, **D**efend.

2   In this we are following the analysis put forward by David Wiggins in his "Claims of Need", *Needs, Values, Truth: essays in the philosophy of value,* (Oxford: Basil Blackwell, 1987), pp. 1-58.

3   One of us was in Athens recently where the authorities had attempted to reduce problems of air pollution and traffic congestion by restricting car usage on the basis of number plates. So, cars with even number plates were banned on one day, and those with odd numbered plates on the next. The result was simply that many people bought a second car.

Select Bibliography

Rather than offer yet another "exhaustive bibliography" in the area of environmentalism we recommend the following texts as centrally important to the project of political ecology.

Ulrich Beck, *Ecological Enlightenment: essays on the politics of the risk society*, Tr. Mark A. Ritter, (New Jersey: Humanities Press, 1995).
  An account of environmental politics in terms of the internalisation of risk. Beck's views help articulate the novelty and challenges of political ecology.
Frances Cairncross, *Green, Inc.: guide to business and the environment*, (London: Earthscan, 1995).
  A generally sensitive, if overly sanguine, account of the possibilities for market-based environmental management. Notable for containing no discussion of social commons style management options, contenting itself with cursory dismissal ("Provided the terms of ownership are correctly specified, private ownership will usually protect resources more efficiently than state or communal ownership", p.252).
Jared Diamond, *Guns, Germs and Steel: the fates of human societies*, (London: Jonathan Cape, 1997).
  An impressive, if controversial attempt to construct a "science of history" on the availability or otherwise of natural resources.
Robyn Eckersley, *Environmentalism and Political Theory*, (London: UCL Press, 1992).
  A clear exposition of the "ecocentric" strand of deep ecology, and one which—if largely inadvertently—reveals its political shortcomings.
Garrett Hardin, "The Tragedy of the Commons", *Science*, Vol. 162, No. 3858 (1968).
  A seminal article for all environmentalists.
John Locke, *Two Treatises of Government*, (London: Dent & Sons, 1990).
  The key text for liberalism and for political ecology. Can and should be read as a defence and elaboration of the social commons style of solution to the tragedy of the commons.
Elinor Ostrom, *Governing the Commons: the evolution of institutions of collective action*, (Cambridge: Cambridge University Press, 1994).
  An important empirical study of nature of social commons solutions to environmental challenges.

John Passmore, *Man's Responsibility for Nature*, (London: Duckworth, 1974).
   A seminal presentation of the ethics of "Human Welfare Ecology".

Jonathon Porritt, *Seeing Green: the politics of ecology explained*, (Oxford: Basil Blackwell, 1985).
   The classic introduction to environmentalism and environmental politics and still useful.

David Wells & Tony Lynch, "The Environmental Foundations of Genuine Socialism" in Tim Battin & Graham Maddox (eds.) *Socialism in Contemporary Australia*, (Sydney: Longmans, 1996).
   Argues for a Lockean account of the nature of environmental politics, and shows how this account, through the idea of the social commons, illuminates the socialist account of justice.

Bernard Williams, "Must a Concern for the Environment be Centred on Human Beings?", in C. C. W. Taylor (ed.) *Ethics and the Environment*, (Oxford: Corpus Christi College, 1992).
   The most sophisticated of the philosophical based attacks on "non-anthropocentric" environmentalism.

Yi Fu-Tuan, "Our Treatment of the Environment in Ideal and Actuality", *American Scientist*, 58 (1970).
   A powerful and much ignored assault on the presupposition that environmentalism demands a radical ethical alteration in our ideas about nature.

Index